The Angels Within Us

Also by John Randolph Price

THE SUPERBEINGS

The Angels Within Us

JOHN RANDOLPH PRICE

FAWCETT COLUMBINE · NEW YORK

A Fawcett Columbine Book
Published by Ballantine Books

Copyright © 1993 by John Randolph Price

All rights reserved under International
and Pan-American Copyright Conventions. Published
in the United States by Ballantine Books, a division of Random
House, Inc., New York, and simultaneously in Canada
by Random House of Canada Limited, Toronto.

Library of Congress Catalog Card Number: 92-90387
ISBN: 0-449-90784-8

Text design by Holly Johnson
Cover design by Georgia Morrissey
Inset: *The New Jerusalem (Revelations 21:2)*,
colored engraving after Gustave Doré/
The Granger Collection, New York
Background: Kaz Mori/The Image Bank

Manufactured in the United States of America

First Edition: March 1993
10 9 8 7 6 5 4 3

To Susan and Leslie, two beautiful angels
who have appeared in this life as my precious daughters.
Thank you.

Contents

Acknowledgments

To my wife, Jan, for the loving encouragement to write this book, for the explorations into the angelic kingdom that we took together, and for the hours of research assistance that she provided—including the sharing of her angel experiences.

To Coe Savage, for her professional expertise and knowledge of the ancient sciences of energies, archetypes, and symbols and for always being there to answer questions and share her understanding.

To the members of the international Quartus Society, for opening themselves and proving that working with the Angels can be an exciting adventure in the process of reawakening.

The Angels Within Us

The Encounter with Isis

For he will give his angels charge of you
to guard you in all your ways.
—PSALMS 91:11

The swirling fog began to dissipate, and I could see the flicker of a light ahead—a darting, pulsating glow resembling a firefly. I paused for a moment to observe, and the tiny flare expanded in size and appeared as a small full moon touching the earth. As I moved closer to the radiance, it suddenly changed into a vertical beam, a pillar of transparent light.

"Are you the angel I am seeking?" I asked.

The soft yet powerful feminine voice replied, "I am the Angel of Creative Wisdom."

3

"Do you have a name?"

"Some have called me Isis," she said, and with those words the pillar of light slowly materialized to reveal the face and form of a beautiful woman wearing a flowing white robe trimmed in gold. "Why have you come?" she asked.

"I seek Greater Wisdom. It is my understanding that you, the Angel of Creative Wisdom, are the channel, the voice, for my Master Self. I know that within my higher nature I embody the wisdom of the ages, yet in my present state of consciousness I am sometimes confused. My thinking has become scattered, which has resulted in errors of judgment. So I have come to ask you what I can do to open the Gates of Wisdom and release that energy to flow freely in my mind and heart."

She said, "You cannot manipulate the Gates. The Greater Wisdom is eternally flowing from above to the receptacle I am, yet I can only give you what you are, for I must follow the sound of your note and harmonize with your energy, even if the tone is restrictive."

"I do not understand," I said.

She gave me a flute. "Play a note," she instructed.

I placed the instrument to my lips, blew across the hole while pressing a key, and a tone was sounded. Immediately I heard the same vibration emanating from the fullness of her presence, the sound seeming to fill all space.

She said, "Divine wisdom has its own note, truly a chord with its own frequency, and as this cycle of life began, my being was attuned to that vibration, which produced the perfect distribution of the Wisdom-Energy through your egoless consciousness, a consciousness in perfect harmonic relation to mine. But in time you changed the tone, and as I am subjective to you, I had no choice but to follow your pitch, which became increasingly discordant. From a cosmic perspective you committed adultery with me. I was the victim of your adulteration; with your energy projections you made me inferior, impure."

I was stunned by this revelation, and it took me a moment to regain my equilibrium. "What can I do? How can I rectify the situation?"

"Play the right note," she said with a touch of impatience in her voice. "Your present sounds are the result of failing to unite the force of love with the energies of will and understanding, and you are applying what you know to the phenomenal world of effects rather than to the inner world of cause. You are highly mental, and such individuals are outer directed, basing decisions on reasoning and rational thinking. Thus the goal is always to attack the illusion—but the opposite of illusion is intuition."

She touched the top of my head, and suddenly I was in a whirlpool of color and sound, falling free through spinning faces, symbols, and numbers. I could hear her voice in the distance: *"Regardless of what your mind tells you, what does your intuition say?"*

My career in the corporate world passed before me, pausing at intervals to show a particular scene with two paths superimposed over the picture. I was asked again, *"Regardless of what your mind tells you, what does your intuition say?"* And then I heard two voices, one harsh and hurried, the other soft and gentle—crossed telephone wires with two parties speaking—and on the screen I was walking the particular path that I had chosen, and I saw the results of that decision. Then instantly the scene changed, and I was shown what would have happened if I had listened to the other voice and chosen the different path. The movie with two endings continued, moving from business to family life to social encounters to the satisfaction of personal desires.

"Open your eyes," she said.

She was standing before me again in all her radiant splendor. "Do you understand," she asked, "that in many of the scenes you were misinterpreting an outer situation—that you were seeing through false eyes something that did not exist? Through the vibrations in your consciousness you were sending me signals of hostility toward your work, antipathy regarding certain aspects of your family life, an aversion to many people, and even a mild revulsion to your world in general. You forced these sour notes on me, notes that were the antonyms of love, which removed one of the tones of my harmonious chord and produced discordance for you."

I opened my mouth to say something, but she held up her hand and continued. "You also adulterated another splendid tone when you let strength of purpose and determination be replaced with irresolution and vacillation. You have free use of divine will, a truth that you certainly forgot. And the third tone of my chord, the light of understanding, was dominated with insensitivity, aloofness, and unresponsiveness, and I had no choice but to replay these defects on the screen of your world."

"You are saying that your note is actually a chord made up of three tones—Love, Will, and Understanding—and that when these tones are blended, the sound of wisdom is heard?"

"Yes! Wisdom in the form of sudden insights, a sharpened intuitive sense, the guidance to solve specific problems, and the imparting of spiritual truths for the unfolding of consciousness."

I asked, "What would be the quickest way for me to reclaim the divine chord of wisdom and free you to do the work that you were created to do?"

"Know your true nature and hold your mind focused on that highest aspect of your being until it is realized. The more you are infused with the energy of your divine mind, the greater the restoration of the chord of wisdom. I would also suggest that you work with the powers of Love, Will, and Understanding—the specific energies represented by these angels—to harmonize your consciousness with the reality of my energy. Just remember that Wisdom is one of the foundation stones of mastery in your world."

I felt that our meeting was drawing to a close, and I was about to thank her for the information provided when a book suddenly materialized in her hands. I asked, "What is that?"

"It is your book. You cannot take it with you into the phenomenal world, but you may peruse it here for a few moments."

She handed the book to me, and I opened it to the first page. There in bold letters was my name and today's date. As I quickly scanned the pages, I realized that this was the book of my life from this day forward, and the waves of joy and excitement rolled through me to where I could hardly catch my breath. "This is wonderful," I said. "I couldn't have imagined anything so fulfilling. It's fantastic!"

She gently removed the book from my hands. "I'm sorry. What you have read and seen with your mind's eye will never come to pass . . . unless, until, the unconquered personality defects that you have projected onto me are transmuted and I am free—free to reveal to you the kingdom of heaven. Leave now. You have much work to do. And remember, play the right note."

Introduction
to the Angels
of the Kingdom

The universe is a macrocosm of creative energy and power, and every man, woman, and child is the epitome of this totality of the cosmos. Within your individualized energy field, the microcosm called *you*, are twenty-two Causal Powers, or angels, that control your conscious behavior and govern the manifestation of all forms and experiences in your personal life. Their existence has been taught since the beginning of spiritual brotherhoods and philosophical societies thousands of years ago. In ancient Egypt the twenty-two Powers were shown as hieroglyphs representing the laws of all phenomena, and one of the volumes saved from the burning library of Alexandria contained detailed descriptions of these angels.

This universal knowledge was pictured symbolically as the twenty-two major trumps of the tarot, a pack of seventy-eight mystical cards that were discovered in Arabia by the Knights Templars—a secret order of warrior monks who played a major role in the crusades. According to Manly P. Hall, founder of The Philosophical Research Society, the Templars took the cards back to Europe and, "to avoid persecution, concealed the arcane meaning of the symbols by introducing the leaves of their magical book ostensibly as a device for amusement and gambling."[1]

These angels can also be found in the Tablet of Isis, which formed the altar before which Plato was initiated into the Greater Mysteries in the Great Pyramid of Egypt. On the tablet, also called the Bembine Table, appear carved figures called "vehicles for the distribution of the creative influences . . . the divine creatures that aid the Father Mind . . . the gods of the spheres."[2]

They are found in esoteric astrology, too, as represented by the twelve signs of the zodiac, the sun, the moon, and the eight planets (Earth not included), for a total of twenty-two. These are the living Governers of Life, each controlling a Gate, or opening, leading to the phenomenal world— conditioning and determining all outer expression.

The Divine Agents are also found in the study of Cabbalism, the Secret Doctrine of Israel. Here they are known as the twenty-two sounds produced by God to be his ministering angels, established to govern all outer form.

And they are the angels called the "reapers of the harvest" in Matthew 13:39, and the "mighty angels" of Christ in Second Thessalonians 1:7.

In the wisdom teachings these Causal Powers are called by many names including Agents, angels, Conscious Thoughtforms, Creative Energies, Devas, Fathers, Fountains, Gates, Governors, Hands of God, Lords, Shining Ones—and more recently in the analytical psychology of Carl Jung—archetypes. I prefer the term *angels*—those, according to the *Metaphysical Bible Dictionary*, who "guard and guide and direct the natural forces of mind and body, which have in them the future of the whole man."[3]

According to H. K. Challoner, an English artist and esoteric philosopher,

> The Christians have always believed in incorporeal beings such as angels, the Hindu Yogis and mystics in devas. . . . [They] are not only vitally involved in the ordering of our destiny, but are the wielders of mighty spiritual forces employed in the very building and sustaining of the Cosmos itself. The devas, in fact, may best be described as centers of force and intelligence who, under the direction of yet greater intelligences, carry out the functions of those particular offices to which they have been allocated. Indeed they are ever ready to aid and give to [the individual] according to the measure of his receptivity. . . .
>
> To them all is vibration. It is their language, their keynote, the manifestation of God Himself. They dwell in a

realm of ecstatic beauty and love, a realm of music visible in glittering, transient shapes, of colour audible in waves of exquisite sound; of perpetually whirling atoms of matter, changing, coalescing, separating in response to the propulsions of the creative energy which the devas live solely to express.[4]

Edwin C. Steinbrecher, an astrologer, metaphysician, and author of *The Inner Guide Meditation*, says that these are "living energies that contain ideas and information, specific patterns of instinctual behavior and thought. They are the energies which somehow attach themselves, without our conscious awareness, to everything we meet in the world we call real. [They] are the life energies that pour out of each of us unceasingly night and day . . . influencing everyone in our lives and causing us to be influenced in return."[5]

You may wonder at this point why I call these forces angels—particularly since they are capable of expressing themselves either positively or negatively. Look at it this way: The Causal Powers are extensions of the Spirit of God within each individual. They are divine thoughtforms operating under the Law of Free Will, which means that they are subject to the energy that we are consciously or unconsciously radiating. And through the adulteration of fear, guilt, anger, futility, and other characteristics of ego, we can literally change their nature. We can divert their divine intentions and restrain and paralyze their expressions.

Each angel has a cosmic duty to function as a vortex, through which it emits the true nature of its being—abundance, loving relationships, success, harmony, or whatever its specific assignment may be. Its role is to serve you, which means that you can override its primary nature and function and create your own reality for it to follow.

Remember that the nature of the angels represents all that is good, true, and beautiful, and unless their energies are defiled by the ego, you will experience those optimal qualities in your life. When your consciousness is attuned to the angel's higher vibration, you will be loved, loving, creative, prosperous, energetic, decisive, wise, intuitive, understanding, joyful, victorious, harmonious, discerning, confident, strong, patient, protected, courageous, imaginative, enlightened, whole, successful, anchored in Truth and wonderfully free—as you were created to be.

So if your "reality" includes problems, restrictions, limitations, and character weaknesses, it simply means that you are projecting false images onto these living energies. They in turn replay those misconceptions on the outer screen of the phenomenal world, and they will continue to project a negative appearance until the energy of manifestation is changed *at the point of expression* within your consciousness.

Before you meet with each angel to solicit cooperation, there are four preliminary steps that are of critical importance. If you have created a mutation in any particular angel through projections of fear, judgment, condemnation, or guilt, direct contact now could well lead to intense internal conflict.

A healing in consciousness must be the first priority, a cleansing of mind and heart so that all detrimental projections can be withdrawn and the energy blocks dissolved.

To quote Challoner again, "man stands indeed upon the threshold of discoveries, of revelations, of the attainment of powers such as have not been known since the days of the Atlantean Race. And herein lies his danger. Unless, this time, he is morally strong enough to control these forces and develop that spirituality of outlook essential to all those who wield great power, once again he will be overwhelmed. . . . Should any seek to use the devas with deliberate intent for selfish or destructive purpose, let him beware!"[6]

Working with the Angels can be a wonderful adventure in cocreation, so let's begin the healing process now by first forgiving yourself for all your miscreations. Actually it really wasn't you who miscreated; it was a false belief, or thoughtform, called *ego* which is nothing but a part of the great illusion in your life—yet ego-action can leave emotional wounds that must be healed. In forgiving yourself you are simply calling in the Energy of Correction, the Law of Adjustment, to transmute the old erroneous patterns and eliminate the ghosts of another time.

Scan your consciousness, and if something from your past comes up that triggers a feeling of shame or self-condemnation, bring the whole scenario into full view and cast the entire memory-image upon the Love of God within you. Do not attempt to push it further down out of mind. That is repression. Give it up to Spirit and let it be burned away. Keep pulling up all the old sin-fear-guilt roots and tossing them on the Holy Fire within, and keep at it until you feel clean and clear again. Understand that it is impossible to release any thought or feeling to Spirit for transmutation without divine action taking place.

The second step in the restoration of relations between you and the angels is to look at the personality problems that you may be experiencing—fear, deception, dishonesty, anger, arrogance, confusion, stubbornness, feelings of futility, jealousy, impatience, resentment, low self-worth, and so on. Also take note of the negative appearances in your life, such as financial lack, family discord, sexual problems, inability to have lasting relationships, sickness and ill health, legal challenges, and business and career failures. This evaluation will help you to see which angels have suffered the greatest adulteration. (See the "negative traits" and "energy blocks" in Appendix A.)

Once you have your trouble spots pinpointed, you are ready for the third step: a *total* surrender of your mind, emotions, body, and personal world to the Spirit within—holding nothing back and giving up everything to and for God. Cut the cords on all negative personality traits from the analysis above and empty yourself of everything that even resembles the third-dimensional human nature. Remember that as you do this, the Law of Adjustment, the correcting principle of a person's divine nature, a purifying energy radiating from one's spiritual self, immediately goes into action. Everything that you truly and sincerely surrender is corrected on the inner planes of consciousness, and the ego projections are withdrawn from the angels.

Once you begin to feel more of the spiritual vibration in consciousness, you are ready for the final step before making contact with the angels, which is to meditate and bring into your awareness the presence of the indwelling Spirit of God. This *must* be done before attempting any visit to the inner kingdom. Contemplate the protecting power of your Holy Self and *feel* the "everlasting arms" surrounding you. Then ask Spirit to guide you into deep inner consciousness—to personally escort you to meet with the particular angel of your choice. Feel the presence of Spirit's Love, Wisdom, and Power enfolding you for the journey within, and see and feel Light all around you as you walk through a winding tunnel.

At a certain point you will see a light up ahead, and you will know that you are approaching the angel. As you draw close to it, notice as its light begins to take on the form and appearance of a physical being, either male or female. Look into its eyes and, with great feeling in your heart, express your love and gratitude and feel its love in return. At this point you may ask it any question that comes to mind, but one that I would suggest is What can I do to assist you in your work of manifesting perfection in my life? The answer may surprise you, but whatever it is, be sure to write it down in your spiritual journal. The angel will also ask you what it can do for you, so be prepared to answer lovingly and forthrightly.

Understand that although contact with the angels begins in your imagination, it is not simply an imaginative exercise. *Imagination* means "the power to picture mentally," so you are using creative thought to take you into the inner planes, where your sense of vision will reveal these Agents of

Cosmic Law. And *they are real*! Plato called them Minor Gods, and according to Dr. Douglas Baker, English author and teacher of Ancient Wisdom, founder of the College of Spiritual Enlightenment and Esoteric Knowledge in England, "their bodies are formed of the Elemental Essence of the Kingdom to which they belong, and are flashing and many-hued, changing form at the will of the entity. . . . They are the active agents of the Logos, carrying out all the details of [the] world-plan."[7]

Each angel is profiled in one of the next twenty-two chapters.

Each angel has been given a name relating to the mythological god who possessed comparable powers, and to the master teacher in the ancient schools of Wisdom who assumed those powers in ritualistic dramas of initiation. However, certain angels may prefer a name other than the one designated. It does not matter as long as the communication channels are clear. The Angel of Spiritual Understanding asked that I call him Magnus, and Spiritual Strength and Will suggested the name Pyra. Be flexible and work with them as you would a friend who wants to be known by another name.

In meeting with the angels you will notice that they do not always take the same form and shape. As your projection on them changes, they will appear differently. Sometimes they are so blocked by the ego that you can only see a dim, hazy outline. I have also seen some of them change from a shining light to a form resembling a human being, then into a symbol (cube, triangle, etc.), and back to human features.

If you are confused as to which angel to contact in a particular situation, ask your divine consciousness to direct you to the appropriate one. During your session with the angel do not be surprised if he or she calls in another angel for participation in an experience. If this happens, ask the first angel to introduce you and explain why a partner is necessary.

Talk with the angels. Have conversations with them; ask questions, listen. You may also be shown what appears to be a scenario, as a film projected on a screen. Watch the "movie" carefully and do not hesitate to ask what it means if you are not sure.

After your first meaningful contact, the angel will continue to work with you below your level of awareness and a message may come into your conscious mind at any time. Listen to the transmission, accept it, and offer your gratitude. I also feel that it is important to write down what you have experienced during each encounter and meditate on it. What is communicated to you may not be clear at first, but the messages always have meaning and can be understood through contemplation. An angel may also appear to you in a dream. Write the details in your journal upon awakening and discuss the dream with the angel during your meditation time. You can usually tell the angel responsible by the subject matter of the dream.

After there is a period of familiarity with the angels, call in The Council of Twenty-Two and have a roundtable discussion of your life. Ask how you are progressing and what you need to do to further distance yourself from ego pulls. You will find it fascinating to hear them discuss you among themselves, as though you were not there. The key here is courtesy—to conduct yourself as you would in a conference room of highly skilled professionals who are working on your behalf.

You will also enjoy looking for symbolism of the angels in movies, while on a walk in the woods, at social gatherings—anywhere you may be, alone or with other people. They delight in teaching through symbolic action and so-called coincidences. The book that fell out of the bookcase, the bird call that sounded like a word, the shape of a particular cloud, a stopped-up drain, a telephone ringing with no one on the other end of the line, finding something that had been lost for years—the possibilities are endless. Be alert. Something may be happening around you right at this moment.

It is important that you read and study this book in the proper sequence, beginning with chapter one and continuing through to the end without skipping around. This particular order in the presentation of the angels will evoke a progression of responses in your consciousness, one building on the other, leading to a deeper level of understanding and a higher degree of self-realization.

Although this teaching is highly esoteric, it is also intensely practical— which means that the principles must be *practiced* if you are to receive their full benefit. It involves a journey in spiritual development, one with rich rewards for the dedicated traveler.

By joining me in probing these manifesting energies you will greatly accelerate the entire reawakening process.

Enjoy!

ONE

The Angel of Unconditional Love and Freedom

In much of the literature incorporating the teachings of ancient wisdom, the first expression, or outpouring, of Supreme Being is said to be Love, which became the Force and Energy of Creative Power. Thus this first angel is the source of all powers and the cause of all manifestations.

On the Isiac Table, which formed an altar for the initiations of one of the Mystery schools, ancient schools of wisdom, the archetype representing the Energy of Love is depicted as the first emanation of divine mind, or Supreme Being. Astrologically the energy of this angel is represented by the planet Uranus, the symbolism of which is directly related to the unfolding of spiritual consciousness and the initiation into a higher order of life through the Power of Universal Love and the Force of Freedom.

In the tarot this angel is symbolized by the card numbered zero, while the twenty-one major trumps represent manifesting aspects, expressions, or emanations of the zero card. Its name is the Fool, which is paradoxically very appropriate. For example, just imagine what an ordinary person would think if he or she overheard someone say, "No matter who you are or what you have done, I love you. I love you as my Self with no strings attached. You are free, and I have no concerns about you, for you are the Holy Light of God and you possess the Kingdom. We have no obligation to one another except to give and receive love. And through this love we rise above our personal needs, our selfish desires, radiating our love universally for the good of all."

How foolish something like this would seem! An honest response to such "naive" comments might go something like this: "If I followed that kind of thinking, I would have to stop criticizing people and conditions. I couldn't wear my feelings on my sleeve anymore, and I would have to give up my rigid expectations of what other people should do and say and how they should act. I'd have to stop meddling in the affairs of others even though I have a better idea than they of what's good for them."

It has been said that the entire mystery of the tarot is wrapped up in the symbolism of the zero card. This is because unconditional love is God-like, and to most human beings both God and Love are an enigma.

When the angels were discovered by mystics eons ago, it was recognized that the master of these Causal Powers was Love—not human love, but divine, Unconditional Love, the very energy that created the cosmos. It is the First Principle, which reveals and sustains all reality. Freedom is associated with this angel in order to emphasize the *unconditional* aspects of divine love and thus clearly to differentiate between the human sentiment called love by the lower nature and the unlimited, unfettered, unbounded Love that this angel represents. The Force and Energy of Unconditional Love is totally and completely free, while the conditional love of human nature tends to confine and restrict both the loved one and the lover himself. The human personality, in its desire to be loved, will attempt to evoke this emotion in others, but it loves in order to be loved—the strings are eternally attached—which produces an obligation in others to meet selfish motives. Such love is manipulative and binding, whereas Unconditional Love is open and without bounds.

Since the time of our "fall" into material consciousness, it has not been human nature to love unconditionally, yet that is the only love that our divine soul knows. And that love is eternally radiating into every mind and heart as an angel of the soul, distributing the love energy and working to free each individual from the grip of ego.

The Chinese mystics called this the Tao. To the Hindu students of the Mysteries it took the name of Krishna. In the Western schools he was known as the Master of Heaven.

The Tao Te Ching teaches that each individual is part of the unified and harmonious universe governed by one eternal principle, which is Tao.

This ancient philosophy has as its central theme "Do nothing, and all things will be done. Move into the Absolute Tao and find your peace there." When we move into the Energy of Absolute Love, we will find that Reality is being revealed through us at every moment. If we try to do it through ego, we only create phantoms.

In one of my earlier books I referred to Love as "the final and ultimate mystery" and told about an old man appearing in one of my dreams with this advice: "If you will only love more, all limitations in your life will vanish."[1] Love truly is the energy of transformation.

When you take the time to think about what Love really is, you can begin to understand the awesome power of the Angel of Unconditional Love and Freedom—God's Hand of Love—right within your own energy field. When this angel is free of ego projection, you are truly a radiating force for good, and anyone within the range of your radiation is lifted to the divine standard of wholeness and harmony. You will know that Universal Love is flowing freely in and through you by the total absence of fear, guilt, and any feelings of repression and restriction in consciousness. If you are experiencing these negative feelings, it means that you are screening out this angel's divine influence, specifically through the act of judging other people and conditions *based on appearances*. Let's take a closer look at what this means.

Anything that is seen as solid and tangible in the physical world—either now or imagined as coming into view at some point in the future—is an appearance. In the spiritual sense it is an "illusion" because it is subject to change; it has a beginning and an end, therefore it is an effect. And the only power in an effect is the power given it by the observer in the course of judging. This process of judging by appearances severely impedes the action of the Love and Freedom Angel.

When we are determined to see only the highest qualities in ourselves and others, we free this angel to dissolve the fears that have held us in bondage. Look at your fears now. Everything that you could possibly be afraid of is nothing but an effect, and that includes people, places, and things. Yes, *people*—you and everyone else who appears as a physical form—are only a shadow of the Truth. Remember that an illusion can appear real, but it is not *Reality*. The physical body, the mind, and the emotions are mutable and impermanent, only appearing to be substantial. Can these shadows hurt you in any way? Only if you give them the authority to do so, and this transferring of power means that you have *mis*judged them, again obstructing the angel who "creates new form and vivifies all things."

Are you afraid of financial insufficiency in your old age, of the sudden appearance of a particular disease in your body, of some calamity befalling you, of losing your loved ones? Is there a fear of failure, loneliness, accidents, death? Identify your fears and face them—and see exactly what you are focusing on, what appearances you are judging. If you made a list of 101 fears, they would represent 101 conditions, situations, and "things" *which have no existence* except in your mind. The Tibetan master, D.K. (Djwhal Khul), who provided the material on Ageless Wisdom for the books written by Alice A. Bailey, has said, "The power of fear is enormously aggravated by the thoughtform we ourselves have built of our own individual fears and phobias. This thoughtform grows in power as we pay attention to it, for 'energy follows thought,' till we become dominated by it."[2]

Why be dominated by something that is not real? For years Mary lived with the idea that she would die a violent death because of a dream she had as a young woman. As time passed, the vision grew stronger—the thoughtform was growing in Power through her attention to it—until almost every aspect of her life was controlled by this fear, and Love was replaced with resentment and hostility. But "by chance" Mary discovered a metaphysical book, one that momentarily lifted her above her fear to show her the trend of her consciousness. It does not take a metaphysician to know what the end result would have been if she had not withdrawn her judgment, taken back her authority, and transmuted this thoughtform through the power of Love.

What about fearful situations that are pressing on you right at this moment, ones that are very real in terms of your life experience? Regardless of how genuine and factual each situation seems, you are only dealing with appearances—and it is up to you to decide how much power you want to give them.

Take for example the problem of not having enough money to meet one's obligations. George grew up during the Depression, and throughout his childhood there was constant talk of lack and limitation. A poverty-level consciousness pervaded his home. His mother called attention daily to the empty food cabinet and complained about not having enough money to buy groceries and pay the rent. George carried this deep-seated memory into adulthood, and there was never "enough," regardless of how hard he worked, scrimped, and saved. Then one Sunday a friend took George to a lecture on invisible Cause and visible effect—the idea that all forms and experiences in the outer world are the result of consciousness. It changed his thinking—and his life.

Even though money is a powerful spiritual asset, it is still an effect, a temporary form. George's fear was based on what he believed to be an insufficiency of supply to meet his needs. He was focusing on the shortage of effects, and by doing so was embodying the idea of lack in his consciousness—not understanding that a consciousness of lack attracts more lack. This state of mind produces fear and shuts down the master Energy of Love, the very energy that maintains the pattern for that which is to appear as a full measure of material form. It was a squirrel-cage kind of existence that was finally overcome when George realized that effects simply mirror a person's mental and emotional nature—and that a consciousness filled with love will result in an all-sufficiency of every good thing through the patterns of reality within.

Dr. Douglas Baker writes that "the Wisdom of the Ages has always said that *all is energy and vibration*. When energy manifests as matter it produces illusion. . . . Matter is a *very temporary focal point* for energy and that goes for all forms. But underlying all forms there is an energy pattern at a higher level constantly pulling matter into it. This is the real, enduring nature of a phenomenon."[3]

Look at anything in the material world, including your body. All is energy manifesting as matter. If you judge by the appearance of shortages, sickness, risks, intimidation, and danger, you are passing sentence on yourself. You are arresting the Power of Love and Freedom and are calling for even more menacing illusions appearing as substantial. The secret is to move back in consciousness, away from that which is seen, and up to the underlying energy pattern, the vibrational vortex that is "constantly pulling matter into it." And where is that pattern, that vortex? Right within your consciousness. Within the living force field called *you* is the pattern for everything that exists in the phenomenal world—money, home, food, transportation, the ideal relationships, and the perfect body—infinite abundance on the third-dimensional plane.

These patterns, or divine ideas, are like slides in a projector. As the Light-Energy radiates through the slide, the perfect image is projected onto the outer screen of your world, and your life appears "filled full." However, if you are experiencing an insufficiency in any area, it simply means that you have replaced the tray of divine slides with those of your own creation. And this came about by identifying yourself more with effects that seem limiting, rather than with Cause, which is your unlimited consciousness.

The divine slides are waiting to be placed in the projector. Understand that *you* are the projector—your consciousness is the thing that projects! And the creative energy is flowing continuously through your consciousness, so your work now is to see (with the inner eye) the reality of the patterns, to love them with all your heart and mind, and to feel the energy pouring through the patterns and radiating out to gather matter and become substantial. This action alerts the angels that you are now judging rightly and that you have made the decision to have the perfect patterns replace the false images miscreated by the ego.

Every time you see an appearance in your world that seems to be below the divine standard of harmony, wholeness, and all-sufficiency, withdraw your attention from the outer scene and change the inner slide from an image of fear to the perfect pattern of Reality. *Change the slide!* Keep that phrase in mind and tell it to yourself whenever that blip of fear pops in. Then contemplate the Pattern of Reality, see it securely in place in your heart center, your feeling nature, and ponder that master blueprint with total interest and love.

The Relationship Pattern, for example, is filled with convergence points for meeting the right person, for attracting only loving and harmonious people into your life, for healing all individual conflicts of the past and present, for making the right decisions regarding interaction with others, for choosing the right mate.

The Pattern of Physical Wholeness embodies the lines of force to heal, restore, revitalize, strengthen, nourish, and reinvigorate your body and to maintain it in a state of excellent health.

The Abundance Pattern is a splendid collection of power circuits for the radiation, manifestation, attraction, and expansion of financial supply, including the channels (the way) the supply will reach you and the plan for your continued financial support throughout this incarnation.

There is a pattern for everything that you could possibly need or desire in this lifetime, so if you see something "out there" that has even the slightest possibility of producing fear, *change the slide*! And know that each time you do this, you are not only replacing illusion with Reality, you are also freeing the Angel of Unconditional Love and Freedom to do its mighty work of helping you realize your divine identity.

Before we meet the angel, let's enter into meditation.

Meditation

Spirit of the living God within, my precious Holy Self, I totally and completely forgive myself for every thought, feeling, word, and deed of the past. I release everything to you—all self-condemnation, all guilt, and all fear—and I close the door on all that was yesterday.

As I forgive myself, I know that I am forgiving all, for I am everyone and everyone is me. And through the cleansing action of forgiveness, we are all wonderfully free.

If I see anything in my world that is out of harmony, I know that I have simply forgotten my true nature. I have given my ego the authority to think for me, and its thoughts are fearful and repressive, causing me to judge people and conditions. As I do, I pass sentence on myself and bind the conditions in my life. No more. The time has come to break the chains and be free.

My Blessed Spirit, I surrender my life to you, holding nothing back. I give you my emotions to feel through, my mind to be filled with your thoughts, my eyes to see your vision, my mouth to speak only words of truth, my body to be the vehicle for your actions. And if there is anything within my consciousness, unknown to me, that is not in tune with your holy mind, I ask that it be removed now. I am ready to be clean and clear and in perfect harmony with I Am, my divine consciousness.

(Go into the silence now and let the divine cleansing take place. After a few moments continue . . .)

Knowing that Love is the First Principle which reveals and sustains all Reality, I ask you to guide me to the Angel of Unconditional Love and Freedom deep within my consciousness—that I may free this Hand of the Lord to do its perfect work.

(Feel the Presence guiding you through a long, winding corridor. Keep walking until you see a dim light in the distance. With your mind and emotional nature aligned with the holy Presence within, quickly move toward the Light and ask it to take a form appropriate for communication, then look into its eyes and express your deep feelings of love and gratitude. Then say . . .)

Angel of Unconditional Love and Freedom, I have asked that all my false beliefs, fears, and feelings of guilt be dissolved, and from this moment forward I will do my very best not to judge by appearances in the outer world. I will replace all imperfect images in mind with the perfect patterns, and I will dwell on these truths of my being until the full and glorious manifestation is revealed. It is my intention to do everything I can to free you to be all that you were created to be—the master of the angelic realm, the Shining One whose Light appears before each Gate, endowing each angel with the Will of God, the Love of Christ, and the Action of the Holy Spirit. I ask you now, what else can I do in my daily life to assist you in your work of manifesting perfection?

(Listen carefully to the answer and continue the communication as two close friends speaking to each other—and later record the conversation in your spiritual journal. Complete your meditation by contemplating this thought . . .)

All that is within me is now in perfect harmony. The divine patterns are securely in place, and the Angel of Unconditional Love and Freedom is ministering over me. My life is good, so very good.

TWO

The Angel of Illusion and Reality

In chapter one we found that the Angel of Unconditional Love and Freedom was the master of the Causal Powers—the First Principle, which overshadows the other twenty-one—and was represented in the tarot as the zero card. So, numerically, angel number one is the Angel of Illusion and Reality, considered the guardian of the first Gate in Consciousness.

On the Table of Isis this first projection of Unconditional Love was symbolized as a magician with a sign depicting a disk with a crescent above and a cross below. In the tarot we also find that the first card is the Magician. In esoteric astrology the energy of this angel is known as Mercury, and in the wisdom teachings, teachings that originated in ancient times to awaken an individual to his divine nature, it is called Hermes, the messenger of the gods. So let's begin our study by focusing on the esoteric meaning of what it means to be a "magician."

In the sacred academies, schools of spiritual philosophy, it was taught that the entire outer world is but a dream. The Magician is the master of the dream, who uses the energy of creative intelligence to cause the earthly conditions of an individual's miscreations to disappear suddenly and be replaced by the expressions of Spirit. That happens when the angel is totally free of ego influence.

Dr. Paul Foster Case, recognized world authority on the tarot and author of *Highlights of Tarot*, has written, "The number 1 (as represented by the Magician), which is geometrically symbolized as a point, means *concentration*, attention, a limiting of the field of activity. This refers to the practice which is *absolutely indispensable* to all aspirants for Truth. Until you have learned to concentrate you cannot perform the Great Work." Of the tarot symbolism of the Magician, Dr. Case said, "The central figure, by his posture, clearly indicates that he draws power from above . . . you cannot even begin to use the subtler forces of nature until you realize that you do nothing of yourself, but simply act as a channel through which the lifeforce expresses itself. His uplifted wand is a symbol of his ability to direct the natural forces with which he works; also of the Hermetic axiom. 'That which is above is as that which is below.' "[1]

Accordingly we see that one of this angel's intentions is to help us develop a one-pointed focus on Truth, on the one Universal Power—and through this concentration on High Cause to see beyond the illusion to that which is real.

It is important to understand that we are continually "concentrating"—but usually downward. As Frances W. Foulks, spiritual teacher and author of *Effectual Prayer*, has said,

> In the old Adam state of mind we filled our consciousness with a mass of unlovely thoughts that have created conditions like themselves in our body and affairs. We have concentrated, whether we call it this or not, on thoughts of lack, limitation, accident, sickness, death. We have feared, we have doubted, we have let our mind be shaken with emotion, all the result of concentration, for concentration is nothing more than fixing the attention of the mind on one thing. . . . Concentration on one kind of thoughts, error thoughts, has built up a consciousness of error, and these error thoughts have been reproduced in the life as error conditions. Emptying ourselves of these and concentrating on higher thoughts will lift our mind into the Christ consciousness, and this in turn will be reproduced as harmony in body and affairs.[2]

As you well know, this is easier said than done; it is difficult to change a consciousness of error with a consciousness of the same vibration—and this is why we have been given this holy helper, the angel who works with *creative intelligence* to separate the true from the false in our lives. It helps us to use our powers of concentration in the right way so that we may "lift our mind into the Christ consciousness." But remember, the angel can help us only as we withdraw the tentacles of the lower nature from their stranglehold.

In order to release more of this higher energy into consciousness, we need to continue the work of dispelling illusions. Our objective in chapter one was to free the Angel of Unconditional Love and Freedom by withdrawing judgments of people and conditions based on appearances, defining *appearance* as a temporary effect, an illusion because it is subject to change. Now let's see what we can do to banish *mental* illusions caused by misperception and misunderstanding. This action will break the ego grip on this second angel and allow its creative intelligence to radiate through consciousness.

What is mental illusion? It is misinterpretation and misperception, the misapplication of a principle based on lack of knowledge, the inability to grasp ideas and apply them to constructive living. It is an undisciplined mind resulting in fuzzy thinking—and a person with such a state of consciousness is usually a poor communicator, unable properly to express the jumbled thoughts in his or her mind.

A person suffering from mental illusion finds it very difficult to follow the printed instructions for assembling things. He or she also tends to lock the keys in the car, misplace items in the home, burn food through forgetfulness, run late for appointments, get lost while driving in the city or walking in the woods, and make less-than-intelligent decisions in daily life.

I was never very handy at repairing mechanical equipment until I began calling for this angel's assistance. In each case there seems to be a sudden flood of "how-to" information that leads me to the step-by-step solution. This angel has also been invaluable in clearing my mind for the writing of books.

My wife, Jan, has had some interesting encounters with the Angel of Illusion and Reality. In one session the angel told her that he was working with her all the time but that her mind was too scattered, that she was thinking of too many things at the same time. The angel suggested that she set aside specific periods each day to devote full attention to creative expression.

Another time the angel asked her, "What are your priorities?"

Jan said, "Good question, and very revealing. They certainly are not what I say they are."

And the angel replied, "Priorities are where you put your greatest attention, effort, and time. You must not want what you say you do very much, or you would do it. If you want it, you will do what is necessary. How much do you love yourself? What do you *really* want to do? Make the *commitment*. You always do what you want to do."

Jan: "Thank you for the truth. In reality I already have everything. If I am not using everything I have, it's my choice."

On first contact with this angel you may be told to begin working with symbols as a way of integrating mind and brain and opening the flow of creative intelligence. By concentrating on a symbol you penetrate beyond its surface appearance and come to realize its subjective reality. Such an exercise will give you a grasp of the underlying idea of the symbol, its meaning and significance, and through practice you will begin to understand the actual energy vibration of the symbol. It will seem to tell you about itself. Symbol meditation will clear the cobwebs from your mind and bring your immediate personal world into sharper focus, enabling you to be in greater control of your life. The seven most-used symbols for meditation are the circle, the triangle, the square, the circle squared, the lens sphere, the cube, and the pyramid.

Another technique for correcting mental misperceptions is the conscious practice of fine-tuning the mind by devoting a half hour at a time to being *totally aware*. Close your eyes, and with the inner eye see every piece of furniture in your home, the exact placement of objects, the wood tones and colors. "See" the paintings on the wall and describe each one. In your mind's eye walk through every room and notice even the minutest details. Now open your eyes, get up, and repeat the above steps physically. Then go outside and commune with nature. Practice being alert and aware of what is going on around you. Focus intently on the flowers and trees, listen to the sounds of nature, smell the air. Remember, you are sharpening your senses and tuning your mind to operate more efficiently in life.

An awakened one once told me that people do not have to learn how to think positively—what they really need to learn is how to think, period.

As an archetype working within each individual's energy field, the Angel of Illusion and Reality has basically three levels of operation. When it is completely blocked by ego projection and is saturated with the energy of all the unconquered personality defects, it becomes the master manipulator and works closely with the ego to deceive, mislead, and defraud, becoming a cunning adversary to spiritual consciousness. Everything is by degree, so now imagine that this angel has been adulterated by ego energy only to where the ego is somewhat in control. You "know better," but you give in to ego pressure. In this vibration you may be only a little "crafty" in your manipulations, just a bit devious to get your way. Rather than thinking of you as unethical or deceptive, others may feel that your way of getting what you want is simply an annoyance and a nuisance.

Now let's move up the scale to where the angel is separating itself from the grip of the ego. As you begin to be more centered in the Presence and have a greater allegiance to the Truth of your Being, this angel will be sufficiently freed to begin sending you signals regarding outer situations: "Fret not, be not afraid, there is no need for concern, the Light will prevail, relax and move through the situation untouched." You still see the "stuff" out there, but you are not afraid of it. In essence the Angel of Illusion and Reality will help you to interpret rightly, perceive correctly, and achieve a right outlook on third-dimensional conditions and experiences.

As you take on more of the vibration of Reality through a concentrated dedication to the spiritual way of life, the angel is eventually freed to do its magnificent work of magic and miracles, and the outer picture changes dramatically—more money than bills, more pleasure than pain, and all the worries transmuted for joyous living.

Remember that the Angel of Illusion and Reality is the energy of Mercury, which Ageless Wisdom tells us is the mediator between the lower and the higher minds. "When Mercury, the Divine Messenger, the principle of illusion and the expression of the active higher mind, has performed his mission and 'led humanity into the light' and the Christ-child out of the womb of time and of the flesh into the light of day and of manifestation, then the task of that great center we call humanity will be accomplished."[3] Mercury is considered an agent of Active Intelligence, the Holy Spirit aspect of God, and has been called the mental principle. When liberated, the angel uses this particular vibration of energy to illumine individual consciousness and spread the Light of Reality, providing us with the creative intelligence to see the phantoms of the phenomenal world for what they are and to rid ourselves of the blanket of worry.

H. P. Blavatsky has said that "Mercury is called the first of the celestial Gods, the God Hermes"[4]—and you will recall that Hermes was the name given to this angel in some of the old schools, sacred academies in ancient times. Let's see what led to that particular identification. In *The Vision*, one of the Hermetic fragments, fragmentary writings believed to have come from Hermes, and other reference works researched by Manly P. Hall, we draw these excerpts:

> Hermes, while wandering in a rocky and desolate place, gave himself over to meditation and prayer. Following the secret instructions of the Temple, he gradually freed his higher consciousness from the bondage of his bodily senses; and, thus released, his divine nature revealed to him the Mysteries of the transcendental spheres. He beheld a figure, terrible and awe-inspiring. It was the Great Dragon, with wings stretching across the sky and light streaming in all directions from his body. . . . The great Dragon called Hermes by name, and asked him why he thus meditated upon the World Mystery. Terrified by the spectacle, Hermes prostrated himself before the Dragon, beseeching it to reveal its identity. The great creature answered that it was *Poimandres*, the *Mind of the Universe*, the Creative Intelligence, and the Absolute Emperor of all. . . . Hermes then besought Poimandres to disclose the nature of the universe and the

constitution of the gods. The Dragon acquiesced, bidding Hermes to hold its image in his mind.

Immediately the form of Poimandres changed. Where it had stood there was a glorious and pulsating Radiance. This Light was the spiritual nature of the Great Dragon itself. Hermes was "raised" into the midst of this Divine Effulgence and the universe of material things faded from his consciousness. . . .

Hermes next inquired about the road by which the wise attained to Life eternal, and Poimandres continued: "Let the man endued with Mind mark, consider, and learn of himself, and with the power of his Mind divide himself from his not-self and become a servant of Reality."[5]

It was after Hermes had received these revelations that he began his ministry. His teachings continue to be available to you through the Angel of Illusion and Reality, the one who causes shifts in consciousness so that you may see that which is true and false, who helps you to interpret situations correctly, who performs cosmic magic to reveal the good and the beautiful, and who acts as the Divine Messenger, bringing the ideas of Spirit into your conscious mind. It should be noted that the ancients were so enthralled by the inner work of this archetype that they said it would be the one that would lead humanity into the Light. Mystics called it the illuminating principle that releases the mind and enables one to be aware of the divine plan. Such importance was given to it that a Persian Mystery school, or secret society, was built around its attributes. It was called the Mithras cult and became one of the main tenets of the Gnostics.

By removing the personality stain from the first two angels you are beginning to love unconditionally and are finding yourself living with a higher degree of creative intelligence. You are not judging by appearances— at least to the extent that you were—which has lessened your fears and restored some of your power. And your thinking is sharper and clearer. Through concentration you have defined your areas of activity and have ceased to worry about the extraneous, nonessential things in life. Because there is little cause for concern now, you can tell the truth in your interactions with people and not have to resort to deception and manipulation to get your way. A higher consciousness is beginning to work through you, revealing the "Ultimate Way"—and your joy vibration is growing day by day.

Meditation

As I look below, I see the child I was, afraid of the shadows, thus interpreting wrongly, perceiving falsely, and imprisoning my divine messenger, the one who pierces illusion to reveal Reality.

That is all in the past. I am no longer a child living in darkness. I am growing UP, going UP, and in my ascension I see the Light of the world of my divine consciousness and I move into this Light of my Self, the glorious radiance of Spirit.

From this mountaintop of eternal brilliance I look before me and see only the shining beacon of Truth revealing the Reality that has always been.

Of what was I afraid? Whom did I fear? There was nothing in the shadows that could harm me; it was only my reaction to the darkness that bound me to the illusion.

In the light of understanding I see this now, and I will remember what I have seen. From the very beginning my Spirit went before me to create harmony, beauty, and peace, and it forever lives within me, guiding me to follow those same footprints in the sands of time.

Beloved Lord and Master Self within, day by day I am growing into your likeness, and I know that soon, in a flash of Light, the two shall become one and I will know myself as God being me, eternally.

My Holy Self, I ask that you guide me to meet the Angel of Illusion and Reality, the Hand of Spirit signifying creative intelligence. Let us proceed now.

(With the Spirit of God within as your guide, take the inner journey to meet this mediator between the lower and the higher minds and establish a bond of friendship and co-operation.)

THREE

The Angel of Creative Wisdom

The Angel of Creative Wisdom stands at the Gate through which the Energy of Wisdom flows from divine consciousness. As you become in tune with her vibration through a deeper consciousness of your Master Self, the flow into the subjective (the subconscious) and objective (the conscious) phases of mind is increased dramatically.

This angel was known as Isis in the Mystery schools, a name that means "Wisdom" according to Plutarch. Manly P. Hall has written,

The mysteries of Hermeticism, the great spiritual truths hidden from the world by the ignorance of the world, and the keys of the secret doctrines of the ancient philosophers, are all symbolized by the Virgin Isis. . . . Isis was the image or representative of the great works of the wise men. . . . Isis represents the mystery of motherhood, which the ancients recognized as the most apparent proof of Nature's omniscient wisdom and God's overshadowing power. To the modern seeker she is the epitome of the Great Unknown, and only those who unveil her will be able to solve the mysteries of life, death, generation, and regeneration.[1]

As the Virgin of Wisdom, Isis represents a state of consciousness already functioning within the energy field of each individual. An extension of the Holy Spirit, she is a living, conscious energy with the responsibility for supplying currents of creative wisdom, acting as a bridge or channel between your lower and higher natures. When her Power is blocked by ego projection, your mind is easily confused, scattered, and unsettled, leading to errors in judgment. When free, she works to provide sudden insights and an easy flow of spiritual truths formerly hidden from your mind.

In the tarot she is represented by the High Priestess, the Keeper of the Mysteries. Alfred Douglas, a member of the College of Psychic Studies and the Society for Psychical Research in England, and author of *The Tarot*, writes, "The book or scroll she holds in her lap represents the Mysteries of the hidden temple of which she is guardian. To those who are prepared she reveals herself as the Lady of Light who points out the concealed path by the beams of her gentle lunar radiance, and gives freely her patronage and protection. Under this aspect she is Divine Inspiration."[2]

Astrologically the Angel of Creative Wisdom corresponds to the moon, yet her power is due to the sun's rays. The esoteric significance of this is that the moon is a reflector of sunlight; it reproduces the qualities of soul awareness and divine understanding in the receptive mind of the individual.

The Angel of Creative Wisdom can be a powerful ally in the journey to higher consciousness, as shown by the experience recorded in the Prelude. Since that time I have listened intently to intuition rather than to mental reasoning in making decisions. (Regardless of what your mind tells you, what does your intuition say?) I have not always followed the inner guidance, but even my goofs have been a learning experience in trusting those so-called hunches.

On one occasion, when we lived on a lake in Austin, Texas, my mind screamed loudly for the purchase of a boat while my intuitive feeling seemed to advise against it. *All* of our neighbors owned boats, and it appeared to be the ideal leisure-time activity, so I gagged the still, small voice and bought one. I should have listened. Within five minutes of paying the man the money and speeding away in the boat, I crashed into a dock. The only injury was to my pocketbook. But even after the boat was repaired, Jan and I never enjoyed the "thrill" of cruising up and down the lake hollering and waving at the neighbors. It just wasn't our style.

There was also the time when my intuition said to move the Quartus Foundation and the entire staff to the Guadalupe River Ranch in the Texas hill country. My mind immediately had a computer printout of dozens of reasons why this was a totally unreasonable course of action, but this time I listened, and Spirit went before us to straighten out every crooked place in the road and perfect everything that could possibly concern us. It was a beautiful demonstration of right guidance and right action.

In Proverbs 16:16 we are told that "Wisdom is better than gold"—a Truth that must be realized before we can enter into the realm of mastery as a "wise one." Jesus said that "Wisdom is justified by her deeds"—in other words, one who takes action based on the principles of superior judgment is always proved right. Every step taken in the Light is the correct one; every effort made in the energy of Wisdom yields great accomplishment.

This is so because in Truth, You and Infinite Mind are one, and in that oneness the secrets of the universe can be known, including the solution to every problem and the answer to every question. And all the gold in the world could not buy that sacred quality and divine power. That is why Solomon chose Wisdom over riches and honor. With Wisdom he could be and have all things.

Where do you find this Wisdom? Certainly not in the self-created belief system of the ego. Neither is it a part of your reasoning mind, and it is certainly different from that which you call knowledge. If Wisdom is not in your lower nature, then it must be found in the higher, in the vibration of spiritual energy—because that's *what* it is—the pure, radiating energy of the divine self.

How do you partake of its unlimited vision, its divine judgment, its holy discrimination, its clear intuition? By letting the highest aspect of your being take control of your lower nature. And when your true self takes command, you do not sound as foolish nor as irresponsible and your actions do not boomerang to dig a deeper hole for you than you were in before. Your words resonate with the Power of Spirit, your emotions are motivated by love, and each decision is looked upon as skill in action. With the energy of Wisdom circulating freely, lack is transformed into abundance, illness to wholeness, failure to success, harmfulness to harmlessness, futility to fulfillment. No wonder the early sacred academies were called schools of wisdom!

Pythagoras said that wisdom was the understanding of the source or cause of all things and that once the student was in harmony with the Cause, all things would be added in the world of form. Jesus said basically the same thing five hundred years later with his admonition to seek the Kingdom first and all things would "be added." So the key seems to be an understanding of our source, the kingdom of consciousness that was God's great pleasure to give at the beginning of time.

In tracking the path leading to wisdom you need only look UP—to that point of individualization where God is known as *You*, the divine You, the only You there is. Whatever you call this God-as-You—Christ, soul, Spirit, high self, the I AM, divine consciousness—just remember that it is your higher nature, and it is the only Reality you have. And when you sense it, feel it, and ultimately realize it, you will find that it is the wholeness and completeness of God in individual expression *as You.* Your divine consciousness—in, around, above, and through you—embodies the Will and Power of God, the Love and Wisdom of Christ, and the Creative Activity of the Holy Spirit. It is the very Kingdom of God, the fusion of every cosmic joy and universal good created in the mind of pure being—and that is who and what you are.

Your Holy Self is at this very moment seeking to influence and control the mind, emotions, and body of your lower nature, that is, your personality. And the more that you are *aware* of this divine consciousness, the more its dynamic energies can fill the physical-plane person you thought you were. And when the infusion is complete, you awaken and understand that you embody all the Powers of God and that you are indeed a master mind.

But you do not have to stand at the fountain and wait until the process is complete to start living a life filled with wisdom. You can begin right now. All it takes is a shift in consciousness to put you on the "moving stairs" that will carry you out of the darkness and into the Light. Let's make that shift by planting seeds of Truth in mind. If you will ponder the seed thoughts given below until you *feel* the energy building in consciousness, you will notice that your judgment is clearer and your decisions will seem to be made independent of your conscious mind, with solutions to the so-called problems of life suddenly appearing out of nowhere. That's what happens when the Angel of Creative Wisdom is freed.

Seeds to Plant in Consciousness

I am alive. That fact is my starting point in realizing the Presence of my Self. My aliveness signifies Life, and I *feel* the Life within me as Me. This Life did not originate in my body. It did not come from my mind or emotions. This eternal life force must be from a higher Presence at the very core of my being.

I can think: I can feel. That fact is the second step in realizing the Presence of my Self. I am an intelligent being with feelings, yet I did not create these qualities of life. They must be expressions of a higher consciousness right where I am.

I have a personal sense of being, yet I sense a higher nature, "something" more than human, an illumined mind—unlimited, unbound and free—an overshadowing Spirit watching, beholding, and *being*. This feeling of something beyond my personality is the third step in realizing the Presence of my Self.

I now take the fourth step and consciously rise up into the Presence of my Self. With purpose of mind I lift my consciousness, and I am moving up, up, up . . . higher and higher. The Light is becoming brighter and brighter. I am ascending into the energy of my magnificent divine Self. And now I see the very apex of my being.

It is good to see Me. It is good to know Me. I look at Me and I appear as the Shining Sun, a pure spiritual being, a living Presence, an all-knowing mind . . . and I listen to Me.

Meditation

I am Divine Consciousness. I am Spirit, Soul, and a Body of Light, and within me are all the powers of the universe, for I am God individualized, the Trinity of God in radiant expression.

I embody every idea of creation and I am eternally creating that which is good and true and beautiful. I am the Kingdom where all things exist, and everything in the world of form is an idea in my consciousness, a point of energy radiating outward to express the Will of God.

I am the Law of all that is seen and unseen. I am the eternal Cause of all that appears. Come closer and I will tell you of a life beyond imagining. I am speaking to you, the mind-energy of personality on earth which has risen into my Presence. Listen.

Although there appear to be two of us, one from above and one from below, there is in reality only one glimmering stream of Light. I am You and You are me and there is no duality, no separation except in thought. This magnificent ray of God I AM has varying rates of vibration, and the personality that is listening to me now is simply in the lower pulsation.

These ideas include the qualities of my being and the appearances of my expression, for I am the Law and the Cause of the unseen and seen. The divine consciousness I AM, your spiritual consciousness, is the Law and Cause of all manifestation. I am the Law and Cause of Wisdom, Love, and life. I am the Law and Cause of health and wholeness. I am the Law and Cause of right relations. I am the Law and Cause of supply in all its manifest effects including food, clothing, home, money, and transportation. Nothing good, true, or beautiful exists in the unseen or seen worlds that does not have its origin in my consciousness.

The beginning of Wisdom is to know Me. It is to become consciously aware of Me, and through this awareness I will radiate my very being. Through your consciousness of Me, the higher You, I will work, flowing out into the world to extend the kingdom of harmony. Your conscious awareness and understanding of Me puts you in oneness with every idea in my mind, and these points of energy will express through you to reveal an all-sufficiency of all that is good in life.

Keep your mind on Me. Relax in Me. Know that the greater the consciousness of Me, the greater the infilling of my Self in you, which makes your consciousness a law unto you, reproducing the glory of the Kingdom in your world. Be still and know Me . . . your Self.

I am now aware of my Self. I understand my Self. I know my Self. And I fully dedicate my life to this God-Being I am in Truth.

To know thy Self is truly the beginning of Wisdom. And remember that you have a holy helper who will work with you until the infusion of spiritual energy is complete and the two natures become one. Ask Spirit to accompany you into deep inner space to see this beautiful angel. When you make contact, ask what you can do to assist her in opening the Gates of Wisdom, then add what she says to the preceding meditation, transforming her words into positive statements of Truth.

FOUR

The Angel of Abundance

In the ancient tarot this angel is represented by the Empress, whose symbolism refers to reproduction, multiplication, and growth. She is the Mother Goddess, the Great Mother principle—fertile, bountiful, and nurturing. She stands at her appropriate Gate in our force field and radiates the spiritual essence of prosperity, beauty, luxury, and well-being. As an extension of the Spirit Self she is the vortex through which the creative Energy of Material Prosperity passes, and unless she is blocked by ego projections of human misperceptions and ignorance, she will ensure that you are continually supplied with an all-sufficiency of good in your life.

Astrologically the Angel of Abundance is represented by the planet Venus. In the esoteric tradition it is said that Venus is to the earth what the higher self is to man. The energy of Venus is considered to be the mother of all creative activity, and in *The Astrologer's Handbook* we read that "The strength of Venus . . . indicates the capacity to create beauty, harmony, and material prosperity, as well as the ability to attract the people and things which the natives love and desire to have."[1]

When this angel's power is diffused by the ego, the individual experiences not only financial limitations but also deep feelings of insecurity, family conflict, and sexual and career problems. A belief in insufficiency affects many areas of life, each condition adding more weight to the original denial of omnipresent abundance. Remember that the Angel of Abundance was created by Spirit to be the Agent of one of the primary provisions of the Kingdom—infinite supply. So why do people experience so many unfulfilled conditions in life? Because that Gate is closed, either partially or completely, and the reason for this obstructed channel will be found in the individual's consciousness and what he or she believes about God and abundance.

Abundance is the true nature of God, which became your true nature at the moment of individualization. When the Supreme Being expressed itself as you, nothing was left out. Every attribute of Spirit, including abundance, was given in all its fullness, which means infinite and eternal. It has also been taught since the beginning of the schools of wisdom, spiritual academies of antiquity, that Absolute Being, or God, does not become directly involved with effects—those things that we would call money, food, clothing, homes, and transportation. So we see that the gift of abundance is *creative energy*, the very Love of Spirit, and this energy becomes the thread and fabric of *consciousness*, which results in material form. Again, it is individual consciousness that expresses itself in the phenomenal world.

When you are consciously aware of the Presence of God, the Presence becomes a part of your consciousness, and there is a spiritual infusion. And when you identify this Spirit of God within as your abundance, your consciousness becomes the principle of prosperity. The energy flows into manifestation *through* you, forever reproducing the vibration of your consciousness in the world of form. The main purpose of these ideas is to enable you to work with the higher law—the Law of Abundance—rather than the law of lack, because consciousness is fulfilling itself as law regardless of where it is focused.

If you are currently experiencing financial problems, you are working with the lower law, which was activated by a false belief that you made up and projected onto the screen of the outer world as a lie. You can see now that effective thinking would not focus on the effect but on the *reason* for the effect—to correct the misperception in your consciousness. You have made an illusion a reality, thus giving power to a delusion and strengthening its holding pattern in your life. Let's take a closer look at this cause-and-effect relationship.

Exchanging one ego-produced effect for another is not the answer. If we pray that an effect in the phenomenal world be transformed into another effect, we are believing that the first effect has power over us, that it has become *Cause*, the origin of our unhappiness or discontent. We are saying, "I do not like this effect. Give me a different one, and this time make it more pleasurable." An empty bank account is an effect, and our belief in the appearance of lack or in the unwillingness of God continually to provide for us is the reason for it. Instead of affirming a full bank account we should meditate for an understanding of what produced the original condition of lack in our minds, speak the word for a healing of that mental-emotional condition, and then work consciously with the Angel of Abundance to reveal a divinely prosperous life.

In the process of tracing cause-and-effect we realize that God has nothing to do with our sense of scarcity—that it is our *consciousness* that produces the undesirable experience. And eventually we arrive at the understanding that everything in the outer world is only secondary to the inner world of consciousness, and our focus begins to change from without to within. With our new understanding we cease trying to manipulate substance and to "make things happen" through the power of mind. Instead we reverse our focus and begin to look for the crossed wires in our system, the faulty circuits, the false beliefs and the personality defects—specifically where we are limiting the Great Unlimited, or God.

When I asked the angel for greater understanding of this process, I was shown a world filled with color, sounds, and animation—of people living in fear and desperation, struggling to make ends meet. Then the scenes were suddenly frozen in place, suspended in time and space. It seemed that the sustaining energy had been removed and only a black-and-white photograph of what had been remained—and even the photo was slowly fading to white. To me the significance of this was that "this world," as projected from the ego-mind and seen through the eyes of the human personality, was only a third-dimensional illusion. Yet "the earth is the Lord's," so a world of divine reality must also exist, otherwise the prayer that Jesus gave us is meaningless. And then I understood that when the obstructions and impediments in consciousness are removed through a deep conscious awareness of the divine Presence, the ego's projected effects in the outer world begin to fade and are simultaneously replaced with divine impressions of a substantial nature. As the pure Light of the divine Self shines forth, the ego's projections are burned away, and all forms, conditions, and experiences reflect only the Will, Love, and Vision of God. Now I saw the black-and-white photograph of my world taking on color and animation again, but it was different from before. I wasn't doing anything; it was all being done through me. And the people in the scenes, myself included, were like happy children. There was no strain, competition, or conflict—only ease, cooperation, and right relations. There was an abundance of wholeness in all areas of physical life. Money was a plentiful spiritual asset, freely flowing for use by all, with no emphasis on struggling to get or toiling to have. Abundance was the *natural order* of things because the divine influence of

Spirit was in control. Ego had been replaced by spiritual consciousness, and the angels were free to produce form out of their own substance according to the higher vision.

While contemplating this vision of Reality, I heard, "Understand the meaning of *light of the world*." I thought of the passage in Matthew 5:14, where Jesus said, "You are the light of the world," and for the first time I knew what he meant. Light, energy, and substance are all synonymous—all referring to the creative power of the universe—and that's what we are! Reverse Jesus' words: This world was meant to be *the world of Light*. And since we are the Light of the world, that Light must be turned *on* the world and *in* the world, for where there is Light, there cannot be the darkness of insufficiency, shortage, lack, and limitation. The human race has been projecting the hell of darkness into the world through the misuse of the energy of mind, when all the time we have had the power and authority to extend the Light of heaven into our lives by reclaiming our identity and cooperating fully with the Angels.

Do you understand the significance of all of this? We "can do all things through Christ"—including the melting down and recasting of our individual worlds. But we must first understand that everything seen represents only shadows on a screen, beginning with the body and continuing to the furthest reaches of our personal lives. We can literally change that which *appears* to be real into that which *is*—at least as real as Reality can be on the third-dimensional plane. (As long as there is deterioration of form, we have not reached the highest level of Reality.)

To assume our rightful identity as the Light of the world, we must first remove the lenses of diffusion—the false beliefs—from our divine radiance. False beliefs are fear patterns created by the ego, and when the fears are exposed and dealt with, the old beliefs are broken up and forgotten—replaced with an inner knowing that God is the only source and that a consciousness of God is the Cause of all good things in life. Some exploratory work is called for now to root out and expose some of those misperceptions.

During my early work with the angels I made a visit to the Angel of Abundance and asked what dominant belief was restricting my supply. Here is her answer:

> When you finally moved into your true place, which was a life of spiritual communications, you could not fully reconcile the idea that spiritual work justified abundance. "Enough to get by" was the projection on my energy. In truth, the type of work engaged in has nothing to do with prosperous living. A race thought (a generally accepted thought or idea by humanity) demands that the value of work equals the amount of compensation, which limits the great majority of people living on the planet. Because you are in spiritual work, the value of money in your mind is lessened even more through a false belief that says that spirituality and abundance are irreconcilable. Abundance is

yours regardless of the work you do if you do not equate what you do with making money. Do what you love to do most and equate the money in your life with the endless stream of energy flowing from the source.

Now let's see how this message applies to you. You do not have to be engaged in what would commonly be called a "spiritual career" to have a similar ego projection. The fact that you are on the spiritual path and are dedicating your life to awakening to your divine Reality may have prompted ego to insert an idea in your mind saying that a spiritual life and prosperity do not mix. This is another lie to make you more dependent on that insane part of your personality that says, "Come on, let's do it my way and make some *real* money. You've done without for too long."

The angels are extremely practical in showing us our false beliefs. For example, the Angel of Abundance may be telling you that you are equating a loss of a relationship with loss of supply, that you are taking a failure in one area and superimposing it over your finances, that you are transferring guilt and creating a money debt, or that if you allow yourself to be taken advantage of on one level, this can set up a similar vibration resulting in someone getting the upper hand financially. Now let's examine the trend of your thinking.

Check your Love vibration. From ancient times it has been taught that the mind of God is pure Love and that money is a consolidation of the Energy of Love. Now, it only makes sense that if the tone and pitch in an individual's consciousness is not in harmony with the Love vibration, the energy will be adulterated. It will be changed from the Energy of Love, which is the manifesting Energy of Money, to a vibration of animosity, resentment, hostility, and even hatred. This impure energy cannot be used to manifest money. It will only manifest as situations and conditions that actually oppose and repel money.

What about unscrupulous types and criminal minds who live in luxurious splendor? Remember that it is individual consciousness that manifests in the phenomenal world, and there is nothing that a focused mind-set cannot achieve—and that includes the accumulation of great wealth. But when the fortune is built by the ego-mind, there will be sorrow and distress directly related to the opulent living. If the Energy of Supply, which is pure Love, is converted by an ego-dominated consciousness into the power to accumulate wealth at any cost, this violation of cosmic law will result in retribution in the form of violence, disintegration of the body, or attacks by society's institutional structures leading to financial collapse and possible public disgrace.

Since Love is an absolute requirement in building a prosperity consciousness, I suggest that you do whatever is necessary to stir up the Love vibration. Start with the first and greatest commandment, which is to love your Lord Self with every particle of feeling you have and then to love everyone else as that Self. You might also go to the woods or to your backyard and find something that has little meaning for you. Pick up a rock, and for the next several days practice loving that rock as you have never loved anyone or anything on earth. Develop compassion and tenderness toward that rock; stroke it, speak to it, and tell it of its divine origin and eternal substance.

Once you and the rock are one, move on out to encompass all of nature and repeat the process. Then begin to focus on people. See each individual as a Holy One of God. When you look at people from the Truth perspective, you look beyond the body and see who they really are—the manifest Spirit of God. Then you will begin to look beyond all form and see only Reality, and the Love vibration will continue to expand. The Angel of Love will take it from there, keeping you in tune with the Energy of Money and in harmony with the creative process of the Angel of Abundance.

Look at your grievances. Remember that the blocks in your abundance circuitry can also be points of friction caused by what you have considered to be injustices. *Friction* comes from a Latin word meaning "to rub," so try to see where you are still harboring resentment and antagonism from being rubbed the wrong way. Go back as far as you can remember and take an inventory through the years. Bring to light every person, situation, condition, or experience that struck a discordant chord in consciousness. Now with purpose of mind and with all the Love you can feel in your heart, stir up the gift of forgiveness. Forgive everyone and everything without exception. Then forgive yourself totally and continue with the forgiveness action until you feel free, clear, and clean throughout your being.

See if you are working against yourself in consciousness. When you visit the Angel of Abundance, she may reveal several areas of internal conflict.

She could tell you that the Angel of Success is sending mixed signals to her because of your low self-worth, or that the Angel of Imagination has been so burdened by your downward visioning that she has been smothered with false images.

Tithing, giving 10 percent of your income to where you receive your spiritual nourishment, if done for the wrong reason, is another way of jamming the circuits. Dedicated people on the spiritual path replace tithing with *sharing* with no strings attached and no expectations. "Giving to get" is the Old Testament way. The New Tidings, or the New Testament, say, "Love one another, give and it will be given to you running over, share what you have and you will be enriched in every way for great generosity. When you give for the joy of it, Spirit will replenish everything you share, replacing all that you give with even more than you had—because through your giving you expanded your consciousness of the Kingdom."

Do you see the difference? When you tithe only to increase your income, the Angel of Abundance says, "He's trying to get it by giving it, which means that he thinks he hasn't got it in the first place. He has invoked two laws, one of tithing and one of scarcity. Wonder which one is strongest in his belief system?"

You do not want competing forces. At the same time that you are expanding your Love vibration and seeing everyone as the same Holy Self you are, begin to share from the heart—not to get a return but for the fun of it—knowing that as you give to others, you are giving to yourself, for there is only one Self. Someday the economic system of the world will be based on the concept of sharing. Ageless Wisdom states it very clearly: *To those who give shall be given so that they can give again.* When you move into the grace of sharing, knowing that you can give freely because you have everything now, the ego's projection of insufficiency is withdrawn, and the Angel of Abundance functions naturally to keep you constantly provided with an all-sufficiency of supply.

Once you have done your part in opening the channel, it is time to begin focusing the Light on and in your world—"your world" being all that you survey through the inner eye as your life on the physical plane. See the Light flowing from the deep center of your being and see it pouring forth into a large circle representing everything with which you identify as an individual. Be aware that *You* are the Light of the world, that *You* are the force of infinite and everlasting abundance flooding your world with divine reality. Remember the Pattern of Abundance discussed in chapter one and keep that "slide" in place. The Angel of Abundance will feel the new regenerating life flowing into her and will throw open the floodgates to extend her power of manifestation to literally make all things new in your life.

Meditation

Angel of the Spirit I AM, I invoke your Power and force to clear my consciousness of all false beliefs regarding money, and to open wide your Gate and flood my world with the infinite abundance I am and have. I ask this in love and for the good of all. Let my financial all-sufficiency come forth now for my right use—quickly, easily, and peacefully.

(Bring to mind the divine pattern of Abundance and feel it securely in place in your heart center. Now look deep within and with the inner eye see the divine flow coming forth. See the Light emanating from the Holy Self, shining through the Gates of Abundance, extending on through that perfect "slide" and pouring out to illumine your world with omnipresent prosperity. Work with the flow by radiating your Love.)

I now radiate with deep feelings of love the Light of the world I AM, and I see the golden rays of substance covering and penetrating my world. The divine Reality is replacing the human effects, and I see everything in my world as whole and perfect. My life is good, so very good.

(With your mind's eye see yourself living in joyous abundance. See everything complete and in divine order, with absolutely no sense of need registering in consciousness. Know that you are looking at Reality.)

FIVE

The Angel of Power and Authority

Before we focus on the particular angel that is responsible for the generation of Power, permit me to discuss how critical it is that we let go of the lower nature and move into the higher realm of consciousness. I will begin by commenting briefly on the "awakened ones," those men and women who have realized their inherent powers and who have awakened from the sleep of humanhood, whom Jan and I have had the pleasure of meeting. Each encounter was a profound experience, for we found ourselves discussing everything from angels to Zaddikim (a Jewish term meaning those whose

Power is complete over mind and matter). Some were men, most were women. They were "up in years" by earthly standards, and their appearances were both young and ancient. If you were to see one on the street, which you probably have, his or her face and figure would not have flagged your attention, but something else would have.

That "something else" is the awesome Power that you feel radiating from them and the sense of authority that they exude. You do not pick this up by just looking at them, however. What you see may be a nice lady or a gentle, unassuming man, and an encounter would find absolutely no trace of arrogance, vanity, or pretense. Yet there is a feeling of being close to an intense radioactive force, in proximity to a cosmic power source. What is it that makes these people different? They have reached a high point in consciousness where they have realized that they of themselves are nothing, have nothing, and can do nothing. In essence, they have moved into a different state of mind where the divine overdrive is in operation—that loving, propelling energy of God's Will, Purpose, and Power that flows through to appear visibly as the fulfillment of every need. How did they reach this level? Through a conscious decision to leave ego domination and rise into the Reality of spiritual consciousness.

This divine consciousness is not something that we have to create out of a personal sense of being. We do not disassemble and remake ourselves in the image of God. We are already that perfect image, so our function is to arise and come to our Self, and in this rising up in consciousness we may see with inner vision a door leading to the secret place. That door is within us, and it has also been called the eye of a needle because it represents too small an opening for the bloated ego to pass through. But Jesus told us how to get through it: *Get rid of everything that is possessing you.* Until we do, the entrance is blocked by our own personal accumulation of "human nature." We must slim down in consciousness, which means transforming ourselves by giving up the lumpishness of fear, the obesity of guilt, the heaviness of judgment, and the plumpness of pride.

To understand this process, let's look at the story of a man called Adam (no reference to the biblical character). Adam had been on the spiritual path for years, but he seemed to be traveling mostly through the valleys. There were a few hills now and then where he caught glimpses of the Kingdom, but in spite of his warm and wonderful meditations he was still dodging the arrows of third-dimensional living. Then one day, not realizing the downward slope of his journey, he found himself in a deep ravine, and an arrow found its mark. And another. And then another. The arrows did not kill him; they just made him suffer. One came from the bow of insufficiency, one off the string of an unkept promise, another from the deadly aim of spiritual pride.

This was not the first time in his spiritual life that his vulnerability had been exposed, but it was the last as far as he was concerned. It was a now-or-never situation, and he chose the former. He went into meditation and rose to the higher plane and found himself before the narrow opening leading into fourth-dimensional consciousness. He stood before that door, and in his meditation he called for the Holy Fire of Spirit to burn away the dross. Then he reached deeply into mind and heart to bring forth every feeling of guilt ever experienced to be cast upon the Fire, continuing until every last vestige of that insidious emotion was turned to ash. And he was guiltless, but the arrows continued to fly.

Next he tackled fear, and every insane scenario his mind could produce was released to the Love of God to be dissolved and rewritten by the Infinite Thinker, or God. Finally he felt invulnerable, as all forebodings and apprehensions had been removed from consciousness. And he was fearless, but the arrows continued to fly.

He then called on the Light of remembrance, and he meditated on the glory and grandeur of the Master Self he was in Truth, a Holy One of God. The threads spun by ego slowly began to unwind in the Light of the Presence, and the idea of his divine identity was impressing upon consciousness. But the arrows continued to fly.

Then one day, perhaps out of desperation, he tried to crash through the opening, but found it impassable. He fell to his knees and cried out, "What else would you have me do?" And the Voice said . . .

"Love the least among you as you do your Holy Self, with all your heart, and with all your soul, and with all your might, for the Selfhood is indivisible. This is my commandment, and a second one follows: Commit your mind to God. Surrender your spirit to the Holy One within, and the crucifixion will be finished."

Adam obeyed and searched his mind for all those whom he considered less or least in consciousness, those who had been difficult to forgive, those who had attacked him in the past, everyone he had ever judged as living in the shadows and not fulfilling their potential—even those with a seemingly animal nature who were wreaking havoc on planet Earth. He began to love them all with the adoring intensity that had once been reserved for only the Holy Self within, and soon he felt a bonding with all souls, and the sense of separation dissolved into wholeness.

Now he was ready for the final act. Vividly imagining himself on the cross of the third-dimensional world, secured with the nails of human beliefs deeply buried in the unconscious chambers of mind, he readied himself for the moment of transition. He began to give up everything that had possessed him in this world, and everything that he had possessed, including all the Truth he thought he knew. Taking a complete inventory of his life— the past, present, and future, the good, bad, and indifferent—he surrendered all, even those whose love he treasured with every breath. After every person, place, and thing in the phenomenal world had been released, it was time for the final commitment.

In a matter of moments he gathered all the energy, force, and Power that could be drawn into consciousness, and then he spoke those mystical words of total release: *"Father, unto thy hands I commit my spirit."* It was done, and in Adam's vision he saw the cross vanish instantly and the wall of separation was torn in two, from top to bottom. And he walked into the Light . . . and there were no arrows. There was only deep silence.

There was a difference between the old Adam and the new Adam. Before, everything depended on his own understanding of Truth, on the right thoughts that had to be held in consciousness in order to be outpictured. Even though he had felt the Presence within, he still believed he had the responsibility for working out his own salvation, for discovering the Truth that would set him free from the problems he perceived in his personal world. There was always the search for the missing key that would unlock the doors to the Father's storehouse of all good.

But now a shift in mind and heart had taken place. Through the ultimate surrender Adam had placed his consciousness under the dominion and authority of the Holy Self within that point of Power embodying the Will of God, the Vision of Christ, and the Creative Activity of Spirit. The Presence of God was now able to think, feel, and act through him, and he began to understand that the Will of God was already done, that it was seen in the mind of the divine Self, and that it was being carried forward into manifestation by the outpressing of Spirit. His function now was simply to be of one accord with this divine process.

But Adam's new mode of living as a spiritual being did not mean a retirement from life, for his beingness included functioning in a material world with a physical body. Although the responsibility for the activities taking place in that world were no longer his alone, his true work of living in the Light was just beginning. He quickly learned that he was not to make any decisions or plans, nor was he to be emotionally involved with anything taking place around him, particularly those situations that appeared as pressing needs. He was simply to understand that God's Will had been done, and that the vision of that Will was being expressed.

He was told to be a beholder of God at work while seeing every requirement for physical living being met easily and quickly and knowing that everything was whole and perfect in his life—thus cooperating with the Grand Thinker's thoughts that were manifesting through him. His guidance was also to speak less and relax more, to be lovingly detached, and above all, to practice harmlessness at every moment. Of equal importance, he was told, was to live the identity of the divine Self and all that the I AM represented—to identify with wholeness, abundance, and complete fulfillment in every area of life, and to do this with joy, thanksgiving, enthusiasm, and imagination.

In the process of letting the Presence live and move and have its being in and through him, Adam was aware that decisions continued to be made and plans formulated and implemented, but they took on the nature of spontaneity and he knew that he was being used as a vehicle for mind-action taking place on a higher level of his being. He could feel the power moving through him and he sensed the words of authority emanating from deep within, words that were reshaping his world without any conscious thought from him. It was as though the cosmic forces of the universe were throbbing, pulsating, and expressing through his energy field. But he understood that this was not an activity of his personality, and this understanding protected him from the condescending and self-serving traits that accompany a sense of personal power.

By letting go of the lower and moving up to the higher, the Angel of

Power and Authority had been freed. The divine Power and Authority cannot operate through a consciousness totally mired in third-dimensional energies, but without that Causal Force we have no dominion in resurrecting our individual worlds from the insane destruction of the ego. When we move to the point of the ultimate surrender and make the final commitment, the door to the fourth-dimensional consciousness is blown away, and we are in our rightful home on Earth. And at that moment the Gate of Power represented by this angel swings wide open, and our God-Self has a clear channel through which to make all things new.

In ancient wisdom this guardian at the Gate of Power and Authority in each individual's energy field was called Jehovah by the Hebrew mystics and the Rosicrucians, Osiris by the Egyptians, and Hercules by the Greeks. In traditional Jewish literature Jehovah is portrayed as the God of Israel, the Supreme Deity, but the Cabbalists and later some Gnostics believed that Jehovah was the Power of creation in the phenomenal world under the direction of Spirit. The early Rosicrucians' thought of Jehovah as the lord of the material universe, the one responsible for our physical existence. Osiris represents the material aspect of the sun, which vitalizes the earth—and Hercules is symbolic of the incarnated, yet not perfected, Son of God, whose power transmutes the lower nature to reveal individual identity. This was the Angel of the Kingdom, whose authority clears the channel through which spiritual energy can flow.

In the tarot, the religious symbolism of the ancient Egyptians, this angel is portrayed as the Emperor, the great king of the inferior world and the archetype of dominion. The Emperor is the consort of the Empress, the Angel of Abundance, and works closely with her in bringing the divine thoughtforms into manifestation out of her reproductive energy. As an Agent of the Presence of God within, he controls the energy vortex through which the radiatory and magnetic powers converge, and if not blocked by ego projections, these are released to fulfill the divine purpose. This angel's positive attributes as expressed by an individual are vigor, vitality, and strong decisiveness, with reliance on the Will of God in every situation. If blocked by spiritual pride, however, the person is arrogant, vain, condescending, and pretentious.

Astrologically this angel is represented by Aries, which is ruled by Mars. Aries is the zodiacal sign through which the cosmic power reaches planetary life, and according to the Tibetan, Djwhal Khul, the Aries energy (which comprises the life force of this angel) enables the individual to "express the will to be and do, unfold the power to manifest, enter into battle for the Lord, and arrive at unity through effort."[1] And in *Meditations on the Signs of the Zodiac,* John Jocelyn writes, "Aries is a sign of male power, and it pushes one forward into positions of power through the pioneering of new fields and purposes; here do we find the quality of initiative. The most evident trait of Aries is intense activity, fired by ambitions, projective energy which must take command. . . . Aries purifies thinking and raises thought power, compelling correction and advancing toward truth. The essence of

Aries is the urge that impels persons to new ideas, plans, thoughts, or proposals."[2]

At the beginning of this chapter I talked about the awesome Power that you feel when in the presence of an awakened soul. That Power is the force of fourth-dimensional consciousness. It is the strength of Jehovah, the authority of the Emperor, and the power-to-be of the Aries energy—all of which radiate from the Angel of Power and Authority. This holy helper strengthens the will to serve the divine plan and provides the power to carry you over the obstacles of life. Once freed of ego projections, this angel becomes the inner authority to control the ego, and your life is then ruled by spiritual Power from within. And this radiation of Power from on high is what you feel when you meet an individual with an illumined consciousness.

For our meditation let's work with the *Adam* example, knowing that as we arise and come to our Self, the ego's grip on the Angel of Power and Authority is broken, and the channel is cleared for the free-flowing of the Kingdom.

Become quiet and still as you contemplate the Presence within, and let yourself be taken to that high plane in consciousness where you see the narrow opening leading into the fourth dimension. Follow *Adam*'s initiation into the Light by allowing the Holy Fire to burn away the dross. Review your life and expose all the guilt you have ever experienced and cast it upon the Fire of Spirit, then bring into consciousness every fear that has plagued you in the past and the ones that are rising up to haunt you now. Bring them all up and release them to the Love of your Master Self to be dissolved. Once this is done, begin to ponder the Truth of you—the shining radiance of your divine consciousness, the very Presence of God individualized as you. See the Light and feel the Love, and return that Love with all the feeling you have!

Now you are ready to search your mind for all those whom you have considered less or least in the human family. As each one comes into focus in your mind, begin to love them with the same feeling that you have loved the Presence of God within you. Keep pouring out the love with great intensity and watch as each human face and form is transformed into Light. Continue until you feel a bonding with the entire Selfhood of God—that infinite circle of Light embodying every soul on this side of the veil and beyond.

In preparation for the final and ultimate surrender begin to release everything in your life without exception—every person, everything that has ever possessed you, and all that you have possessed—leaving nothing out. When you have emptied the shelves of consciousness and nothing remains, gather your energy into a mighty force and speak aloud the mystical words: *"Father, unto thy hands I commit my Spirit."* Your crucifixion will be over, and you will find yourself in the Kingdom of Light.

Now you will want to visit the Angel of Power and Authority, an angel worth knowing, respecting, and loving. Ask him what you can do to help maintain control of the ego. Listen to his constructive ideas and write them in your journal. You might also tell him to strengthen your resolve to stay firmly on the spiritual path and to alert you if spiritual pride begins to develop in the lower chambers of consciousness. And remember, this is the angel of enthusiastic action that can propel you forward to achieve even the most "impossible dream."

SIX

The Angel of Spiritual Understanding

The Angel of Spiritual Understanding stands at its Gate of expression to help us grasp, comprehend, absorb, interpret, know, and appreciate the meaning of all things—including ourselves. And one of the greatest services that this energy provides is open-mindedness, an attribute that most of us could use in heaping measure.

Accordingly, the birthplace of true understanding is right within our consciousness. As that dynamic energy begins to work in our minds, we first develop an intellectual understanding of our divine constitution, and as it seeps into our emotional nature, a sense of knowing is registered subjectively. We are beginning to realize the Truth of our nature, but realization is by degrees and it is not until we have elevated understanding to its highest spiritual level that we move into Knowingness—where we know, and know that we know.

Emilie H. Cady, an early 20th-century medical doctor, spiritual teacher, and author of *Lessons in Truth*, has written,

> You may easily grasp with the mind the statement that God is the giver of all good gifts—life, health, Love—just as people have for centuries grasped it. Or you may go further, and intellectually see that God is not only the giver, but the gift itself; that He is life, health, Love, in us. But unless Truth is "revealed . . . unto thee" by "my Father who is in heaven" (Matt. 16:17), it is of no practical benefit to you or to anyone else. This revelation of Truth to the consciousness of a person is spiritual understanding.
>
> You may say to yourself . . . that you are well and wise and happy. On the mental plane a certain "cure" is effected, and for a time you will feel well and wise and happy. This is simply a form of hypnotism, or mind cure. But until, down in the depths of your being, you are conscious of your oneness with the Father . . . you will not have spiritual understanding.[1]

At this point we should inquire as to the difference between understanding and wisdom. In the chapter discussing the Angel of Creative Wisdom we found that wisdom was skill in action—the know-how to solve any problem and the ability to fulfill one's needs. Understanding, on the other hand, is more of a contemplative form of energy, energy that is thoughtful, meditative, cogitative. Understanding brings the conscious mind into greater rapport with the soul, where the realization of our divine identity can take place. True understanding also opens the mind to *harmlessness*, where the motive behind all activity is goodwill.

As stated, the first step in gaining understanding is to become aware of who and what you are and to broaden that awareness to include everyone without exception. It is being conscious of the spiritual principle of Selfhood—the Truth that the Spirit of God is expressing as your individuality, your divine Self, which in turn expresses through your personality on the lower plane. Your divine consciousness, your Self, is God's center for expression, and your personality is *your* channel through which the fullness of the Kingdom radiates. Look at it another way: You *have* a physical body, an emotional body, and a mental body, but you *are* a spiritual being, a Light body, a divine individual. This Truth of you is known as the high self, soul, Christ self, superconsciousness, Angel of the Presence, Son of God, and the Holy I AM. Whatever you call it, it is the presence of *You* embodying the fullness of the Godhead. You are God being *You*! The awareness of this Truth is the building block of spiritual understanding.

From this point your awareness must expand to grasp the fact that at the central core of You, you are literally connected and united with every You, Me, and I in existence on this side of the veil and beyond. Every Self in all the universes is actually one pure undivided essence. As an analogy, it is the light of the sun everywhere present on a clear day or the endless water of an infinite ocean. Remember that the definition of the word *individual* is "an indivisible entity," which means that there is not and cannot be any separation in the Selfhood of God. The "distinctions" are simply cells of consciousness within the one body of God. I am you and you are me, and we are everyone else. Contemplate this Truth.

An understanding of who and what you are leads to loving gentleness and true harmlessness. A new tone and rhythm emerge in consciousness, and your loving contact with others becomes your point of service. You begin to understand people—their strengths and weaknesses, their victories and defeats, their needs and aspirations. Your zealot stance on causes and issues softens because your focus is on the Truth of Being, and if someone does not share your third-dimensional beliefs, you do not feel attacked or rejected, nor do you feel the need to attack or reject others. You practice harmlessness, for true understanding involves identification with everyone as yourself. Whereas before, under the glamour of idealism, you sacrificed the spirit of love, you now see more inclusively and avoid the former areas of misunderstanding. Your stubbornness and separative superiority give way to loving understanding of all parts of the whole.

It is extremely difficult to practice Unconditional Love until the energy of spiritual understanding is flowing freely; otherwise we are going to be caught up in another's pettiness, rigid expectations, and closed mind. But with loving understanding we can see his or her divine value, express Love with no strings attached, and know that "this too shall pass" as the person releases the critical spirit and becomes centered in Truth.

What does it mean to be "understanding"? Think about the meaning of loving detachment while standing in your spiritual beingness. It is putting up your sword and seeing through the eyes of your adversary. It is the development of spiritual empathy—the projection of your own conscious-ness into the consciousness of another in order to understand the person better. All pairs of opposites should do this: vegetarians and meat eaters, feminists and chauvinists, nonsmokers and smokers, alcoholics and abstain-ers, pro-choicers and antiabortionists, liberals and conservatives, religion-ists and atheists, New Agers and Fundamentalists, exercise fanatics and couch potatoes, gays and straights, and any other shades of polarity. Im-possible? No. Difficult? Perhaps. But when you consider that your reawak-ening and remembering of spiritual mastery depend on it, you know that it is time to start moving in the right direction.

You begin with a decision to change your attitudes, and from that changing of gears in consciousness will come the Power to help you see Truth and Reality from the level of the soul, rather than from that of the personality. As an exercise in making that shift, think about those things that distress you in this world, the ones that cause you anguish and anger. Look at rights, causes, and crusades that evoke a hostile reaction in you.

Then examine anything else in your life that is causing strong emotional reactions.

Now, to the extent that it is possible, become very detached from all of the above. Keep working at it in consciousness until you have released everything with an attitude that "it's just not worth getting upset about." Then in your mind see yourself on a stage, and painted on the stage is a long white line. Find the center of the line and see yourself standing right at that point of equilibrium—in perfect balance. Now observe each end of the line, the points representing the polar opposites of everything that charged your emotions. Look carefully at both sides of each issue. In all likelihood there is still a trace of anger or despair regarding your emotional involvement with one of the opposites. That is your personality still holding on.

Turn on your imagination faculty now and see yourself as living beyond the veil—out of incarnation—functioning in your Light body and watching what is happening on the third-dimensional plane. See the battle for hearts and minds taking place below with silent detachment. Remember that we all script our roles to have our experiences to learn our lessons, so what you are seeing is an earthbound stage play composed of people dealing with effects initiated somewhere, on some level, at some time—and they are working with these effects as the catalyst for their learning experiences. But you have nothing to do with it; you are only an impersonal and indifferent observer. Keep watching the production until you clearly see the motivation from each side of every question, and know that you are observing the mind-sets involved through the Light of understanding. You are *being* understanding. And as you let this energy of understanding circulate through your consciousness, you will realize that you are being harmless in your thinking and loving in your feeling nature.

Once you have developed a deep awareness of your Self and others as your Self, and have found that point of universal balance, you are ready to understand more of the cosmic mysteries. You have opened your mind to grasp and appreciate spiritual principles and to delve into—with understanding—the sciences of attraction, color, creation, energy, force, healing, light, manifestation, radiation, sound, and symbols—to name only a few, all of which will enable you to grow in knowledge and to assist others in the awakening process. And remember, you have a holy helper who will be with you on this journey into Knowingness.

The Angel of Spiritual Understanding was referred to in the Wisdom teachings as the Grand Master and the Priest of the Mysteries. This masculine counterpart of the Angel of Creative Wisdom was also considered the archetype corresponding to the Initiator, or master teacher, in the early sacred academies, the one who taught reconciliation, union, and immortality. This Power center within each individual's force field is constantly radiating its energy to create and sustain our experiences in the phenomenal world as they relate specifically to *understanding*. If unburdened by ego, this divine thoughtform will open our minds to receive deep spiritual Truths from our source. However, if repressed by ego projections, we become opinionated, stubborn, and obstinate, with a know-it-all attitude and an unyielding personality.

This angel is reflected in the tarot as the High Priest, or Hierophant. The pillars on the card symbolize the Law of Polarity—the interplay of the pairs of opposites—and other designs represent the union of the opposites and the elevation of consciousness to the plane of spiritual understanding and Reality.

In esoteric astrology the energy of this archetype is represented by Taurus. Alice A. Bailey, author of more than twenty books on Ageless Wisdom, in collaboration with the Tibetan master, Djwhal Khul, wrote that "Taurus forges the instruments of constructive living or of destruction; it forges the chains which bind or creates the key which unlocks the mystery of life. [This energy] manifests as stubbornness in the average man . . . or as intelligently expressed will—actuated by the impulse of love—in the advanced man."[2]

According to *The Symphony of the Zodiac* by Torkom Saraydarian, a philosopher, lecturer, and writer from Asia Minor, considered an authority on energies, "The Eye shining from the head of the constellation of Taurus is the transmitter of that cosmic light which is called 'the penetrating Light of the Path'. I would call it the waiting eye, the light of which shines as a beacon on the stormy ocean of life and leads the planetary and solar pilgrims toward the path on higher and higher spirals . . . those who are inspired by the light of the Eye of Taurus seek to work out the divine Plan, to understand the Will of God and put their divinity into action and expression."[3]

Think about it. Right within your auric field is the Angel of Spiritual Understanding, a divine force, an Agent of Cosmic Law that will create a new vibration of higher understanding at the very point of your objective consciousness—if you will only break down the inflexible patterns in your mind. This energy extension from your essential being will interpret the divine voice and communicate spiritual truths to help you master the lessons of living in this world.

The world in which most people live is not heaven on earth. It is a product of the collective consciousness, which constantly mirrors duality. It is a false world produced by mind, and that is why it is called an illusion. When you contemplate the God Self I AM as infinite supply, wholeness, perfection, creative success, peace, and the essence of all relationships, you are deepening your awareness of the truth of your Reality. And that warm, loving, pulsating vibration in your heart center is the energy of Truth rising to the surface to make you free. How does it free you? The Light of Truth radiating from you reveals the absence of sickness, discord, lack, and limitation—and it does this by dissolving the thoughtform illusion that had been projected by your mind. When you suddenly "get well" or have an all-sufficiency of supply to meet your needs, it is not because God has healed your body or prospered your affairs; it is because the Light of Truth has revealed that there is no Reality to sickness or scarcity. All seeming "miracles" are simply the evidence of God fulfilling the Law of Harmony through your realization of Truth.

As I work with the Angel of Spiritual Understanding, it becomes very clear why the ancients referred to this archetype as the realm of knowledge and insight, one who rules a spiritual kingdom and stands for an important teacher. Ask your Holy Spirit to take you to meet this Hierophant. When you make contact, either through feeling or with the inner eye, express your Love and gratitude for its mighty work. And then ask, "What can I do to assist you in establishing the vibration of spiritual understanding in my consciousness?" Write the answer in your spiritual journal and go to work immediately on that which needs to be done. In preparation for this meeting let's meditate.

Meditation

Most High within, I come before you this day to release everything that is holding me back from spiritual understanding. I give up all judgment and criticism, for to judge and criticize another is to pass sentence on myself, and I choose to be free.

I surrender my closed-mindedness, my opinionated views, my inflexible attitudes, my unyielding personality, for I have bound myself in the mire of projecting my own expectations and convictions upon others, and I choose to be free. As I free them, I free myself, and we shall now walk the Path together as holy brothers and sisters in the Light.

I am a seeker of Truth, and I open my mind to the divine inflow of spiritual understanding. I feel the magnificent energy of Knowingness filling me now. My very consciousness is being initiated into the Mysteries of life, and in this sacred ceremony I ask you, my radiant Presence, to mold me to the divine Will, and let me dwell constantly in the realization of who I AM and in the eternal oneness of Selfhood.

I now accept the mantle of understanding.

SEVEN

The Angel of Loving Relationships

While meditating on the subject of loving relationships one day, I was told by the angel in charge to "think about relationships as applying to the bond of harmlessness and harmony between each and every individual." Of course! Loving relationships mean more than just attracting the right soul mate or finding the recipe for living with someone without conflict, for true bonding must include the entire planetary family. And when I asked what the foundation stone was for any kind of relationship, the reply was "Responsibility—the ability to respond to that which is needed by another without undermining the responsibility that is his or hers to shoulder. This is the key to Right Relations."

This tells us that if two people are going to enjoy a relationship, any kind of relationship—friends, lovers, husband and wife, father and son or daughter, mother and son or daughter, people in the workplace—both parties must be responsible. And this responsibility includes the understanding of what is required for a quality bonding and then responding fully to those needs. Yet this is to be done without violating free will and by not taking away the opportunity for the other person to grow physically, emotionally, mentally, and spiritually. Later we will look at how to do this. For now let's remember that each one of us came in with a soul assignment, and we must not take the other person's place in the School of Life and try to master the lessons for him or her. To take on another's tests under your name is cosmic cheating and will incur karma for all concerned.

A few years ago I heard a mystic say that the creed for the new world must be "We are one, and I am responsible for you." And a friend once said that the ancient meaning of Christ is "to give what is needed." Now we can understand the significance of "responsibility"—the quality of being responsible without meddling so that we can focus on giving that which is needed. But all that we really have to give anyone are the fruits of our own consciousness, which means that once again the starting point in any right and loving relationship is the individual you see in the mirror.

First of all, we cannot truly love another person if we do not love ourselves, and this truth is emphasized and explained in Mark 12:28–31.

"And one of the scribes came up and heard them disputing with one another, and seeing that he answered them well, asked him, 'Which commandment is the first of all?' Jesus answered, 'The first is, Hear, O Israel: The Lord our God, the Lord is one; and you shall love the Lord your God with all your heart, and with all your soul, and with all your mind, and with all your strength. The second is this, You shall love your neighbor as yourself. There is no other commandment greater than these.' "

Jesus tells us that "the Lord is one," meaning that the divine consciousness, the Master Self, is the one Self of every individual on this plane and beyond. We have looked at the Selfhood Truth before, and let's reinforce it even more now. If you took a white canvas and drew golden circles all over it, you would have a crude analogy of Selfhood. At first glance you would see only the circles, but the common denominator of all the circles is the canvas. It represents the universal Spirit of God, and the canvas within each circle represents that Spirit individualized—as an individual Self. The golden circle is symbolic of our awareness of this Truth, and when we look within, we are beholding our divine identity—omnipresence, omnipotence, and omniscience expressing as our individual being.

After establishing the principle of universal oneness, Jesus says to love our Self with everything we've got. With heart, soul, mind, and strength we are to love, adore, treasure, and cherish this magnificent master being that we are. And since our divine individuality is continuously reflecting itself in the personality and physical body, we must not completely overlook the "circle." Although we will not feel the passionate affection and rapture toward the physical-plane self that we do for the Master One within, there should be a deep sense of esteem, approval, and a friendly feeling for the person that we present to the world. That's love too. Remember, there is only one beam of Light. What we call the lower nature is but the unrealized Light at the lower end of the spectrum. If Love can transform the wildest beast of the field, it can surely tame the ego.

The third part of the great commandment is to love our neighbor as we love ourself. *Neighbor* means "another person," and since every other person represents the same Spirit and Self, we are simply being told to love the one Presence appearing as many, regardless of the mask (persona) he or she is wearing. I had a revealing experience years ago of totally disliking a particular person, to the extent that I could see myself inflicting physical harm on him. I found my way out of the dilemma by focusing constantly on the divine person standing in the midst of the illusion. It took several weeks of discipline and dedication, but a metamorphosis did take place—in both of us. The more of the spiritual reality that flickered in his energy field, the more I sensed the Presence within me, and then one day I realized that there was a feeling of mutual Love between us as the Light had broken through and bonded us.

I understood later that what I was seeing in others and receiving from them was a projection of what was inside of me. And this applies to the full spectrum of relationships. As I wrote in *A Spiritual Philosophy for the New World,*

These are mostly unconscious thoughts and feelings, those that have been repressed. But all energy must be expressed in some way, and repressed energy is expressed through projection, i.e. putting it on someone else so that you can experience certain characteristics of yourself in another person and learn from the experience. To be specific, if you say that "no one wants to make a commitment anymore," you are really saying that *you* don't want to commit yourself. And perhaps this is because you do not feel worthy—you are not worth being committed to. The root of this unworthiness could very well be some form of guilt lurking in the depths of your consciousness, a guilt for past wrongs on which *you* have condemned yourself and therefore have to be punished. What you are projecting is "Don't get too close and don't appear interested in me because I have sentenced myself to a life of separation from a loving relationship." The other person picks this up and plays it out for you.[1]

Kenneth Wapnick, a Clinical Psychologist who lectures and writes on *A Course in Miracles*, writes, "What obscures our awareness of love's presence in ourselves and our relationships is guilt. As two people continue to learn their lessons of forgiveness, their guilt correspondingly decreases: the less guilt present, the more love we can experience. It is this love that 'grows' in a relationship. In reality, it is the decrease in guilt through forgiveness that allows the love that always was to dawn within our minds."[2]

Earlier I mentioned the word *karma*, which means action and reaction, or the impersonal law of cause and effect. More karmic effects result from relationships than from any other activity of life. Every thought, word, and action in one way or another affects a relationship, for "the measure you give will be the measure you get" (Matthew 7:2). All that is given returns, so the injunction to "love one another" and follow the Golden Rule is truly a guide to living more harmoniously through the right application of karmic law. By being consciously aware that we always reap what we sow, we can begin to build right relations—with loving thoughts, encouraging words, and constructive action—from the home to the workplace, and everywhere in between.

One of the most famous of the Hermetic principles is *as above, so below*. It is an absolute Truth that deals with correspondences, and it enables us to solve a problem by moving above the level where the difficulty seems to be. Those of you who have practiced the forty-day Prosperity Plan in *The Abundance Book*[3] used this law to reveal the abundance that is already a part of your true nature. If you recall, the key words were *of, as, is*. In the matter of relationships we would say, "My consciousness *of* my divine Self *as* the source of my loving relationships *is* my loving relationship." You can only have what you are conscious of having. As above, so below.

In applying this principle you are moving from effect to Cause, into the creative realm of your Spirit, and you are letting the vibration of your higher nature be the attracting and harmonizing Power. Look at it this way: The place where you are experiencing the need for a loving relationship (or harmonizing a difficult one) is the point of "below." Just up from this level is your thinking-feeling nature, which is the point of "above." On this level you are projecting a vibration of need (not having) and perhaps some friction, fear, guilt, rejection, and unworthiness. As above, so below. However, when you move up to the higher level of consciousness, you tap into the Energy of the Master Self, which moves through your awareness out into the phenomenal world to create the bond of harmony you have been seeking. The new "above" will reveal a new "below," thus proving the Truth of this ancient law.

And do not forget the part that states that "both parties must be responsible" for an enjoyable relationship. When you are conscious of the Master You as the source, cause, and quality of your bonding with others, the Master You takes full responsibility for working in and through all concerned—*to give what is needed.*

Jan once gave a lecture entitled "There Is Only One Relationship." She was referring of course to the relationship with the Master within and was telling us that if we could cease looking "out there" for solutions and devote our time and attention to the Magnificent One within—and love that Self with all our heart and mind—our lives would be filled with relationship miracles. Ask yourself, isn't it time you stopped limiting your great unlimited being? Isn't it time you eliminated all the conditions that you have imposed on the grand unconditioned consciousness of your Holy Self? Regardless of how long you have been on the spiritual path, you intuitively know that the solution to every problem lies within, which means that your life and world can be healed and harmonized by the Lord and Master Self that you are in truth.

As a fearful, frustrated ego you can psychoanalyze every relationship problem until you drop in a heap. And all the time your smiling, loving, joyous, all-knowing cosmic Self is waiting to make "all things new" in your life. All it needs is your willingness to withdraw your ego projections, your dedication to working with the law of cause and effect by casting the right bread upon the waters, and your awareness of its Presence and your recognition that it is the *only relationship*. With your commitment to releasing the fear and guilt and with your understanding of the law, coupled with your awareness and recognition, you are building a consciousness for that which is desired. And soon the bond of harmlessness and harmony between you and "that person" will be firmly established. And it does not make any difference if you don't know his or her name now, because the attracting, right-choice-making activity of Spirit will be freed to do its work. Not only will it bind all right relations, but it will also loosen those that do not belong in your life anymore.

Now let's meet the Angel of Loving Relationships, our holy helper in this particular area. In the Egyptian schools this angel was known as Anubis and was associated with the sun, a symbol of enlightenment and immortality. This divine thoughtform represents the life force of masculine and feminine energies—opposites bonded together and complementing each other in one specialized Causal Power. It was considered "the Agent of discrimination between opposites and was said to be the offspring of Isis,"[4] the Angel of Creative Wisdom.

This living, conscious energy releases a particular vibration to condition us to intuitively make the correct choice in all personal relationships, including those leading to courtships and marriage. However, it does not limit itself only to affairs of the heart. It is a power center that constantly reminds us of the responsibility involved in the exercise of our free will to choose any kind of emotional bonding. If its energy is blocked by our own sense of guilt, unworthiness, or fear of rejection, our discrimination faculty is masked, resulting in poor decision making in relationships leading to unrequited love and sexual problems.

This force was certainly in evidence when Jan had to make a decision regarding her mother. The doctor had called Jan saying that Imogene could no longer live alone and that something must be done at once. As Jan wrote in the February 1990 *Quartus Report,*

The Angel of Loving Relationships . . . is represented by Gemini, which is also my sun sign, and its energy of goodwill, right relations, and cooperation among people was constructive in healing emotional and mental barriers and making the right choices.

John was shown in meditation one of those paint by numbers kits and told, "See, the picture is already there; just paint by the numbers one at a time and you will see it complete." So we decided to paint by the numbers . . . and on the seven hour drive to my mother's house we rode in perfect peace. By phone I had located a well-recommended retirement home in the town where she lived and they had one apartment available. The next morning we toured Colonial Village. It was beautiful, lovingly and professionally staffed, offered even more services than we expected and yet respected the independence of those who lived there. Mother agreed . . . and all the details fell into place. Later, after we had returned home, I called and the lady across the hall was visiting. She said, "I just want to tell you that your mother went dancing last night . . . also this man down the hall is stopping by everyday to escort her to meals."[5]

The Angel of Loving Relationships did indeed help us to paint by the numbers, and the resulting picture was one of peace, joy, and fulfillment for all concerned.

The Angel of Loving Relationships is represented by Gemini, the mighty force that will one day create global unity. John Jocelyn, a spiritual teacher, philosopher, astrologer, and author of *Meditations on the Signs of the Zodiac*, says that this energy is "a linking force that unites and shows relationships, the relations between rhythm and form, between self and substance, and between the self and its neighbors and relatives. Implicit in this symbol of divine wisdom is the perfect purpose of divine love. Love and wisdom are a twain that cannot be separated, and it is in this polarity that there manifests the archetypal light of the Christ."[6]

In the tarot this energy form is known as the Lovers—and again, it represents the responsibility for making choices. The symbolism illustrates duality unified, the male and the female complementing each other.

In addition to the healing and harmonizing of relationships, this angel can be very helpful in deepening your awareness of your divine consciousness in a most dramatic manner, as shown in the symbolism of one of Jan's meditations. She had asked the angel's assistance in creating an experience on the inner plane where she could feel a higher bonding with her Holy Self. From Jan's journal:

> Before me appeared two beautiful, smiling beings. Of course, the twins. They blended as one, as me, and suddenly I was on a green mountain, gently rounded, with soft grasses and wildflowers of many colors. I was dancing, dressed in a white Grecian outfit. I wanted to pick a flower but thought that I shouldn't, for then it would be gone. I bent down and

picked one, and it was still there. Then I heard ceremonial music, and I was in a white temple, open at the top, and I was doing a sacred dance. There was to be a wedding and my dance was to welcome the bridegroom. I saw him enter; there was a form but not a human body. We started to dance a classical ballet, bodies moving together until we merged into one. Then the dance was inside of me. It was wonderful, but I wanted to do the dance outwardly as well. Then I felt myself move outward and dance on the mountain without losing the wholeness, for the lower and higher, the physical and the Light, had merged into one.

We have scores of letters from men and women who have worked successfully with this angel, and when a friend of mine called to say that she had found Mr. Wonderful, I assumed that she, too, had released the energy of this Causal Power to attract this love into her life. When we met for dinner one evening, I was silently contemplating what an excellent match the couple seemed to be and how happy they were, which perhaps was my way of congratulating the Angel of Loving Relationships for a fine job. It was at that point that I heard the words "This is not a lasting relationship," yet my intuition told me not to say anything to her, that I must not become involved in her opportunity to learn a valuable lesson and grow from it. Less than six months later they parted company, wiser for the wear.

Contact and communication with this angel could very well have saved time, frustration, and financial resources—with sufficient teaching from within to preempt the necessity of a third-dimensional lesson.

The Angel of Loving Relationships does have an assignment of paramount importance. Standing on the rim of consciousness, it communicates its vital messages through our intuitive nature to help us to be discriminating, make the right choices, heal emotional and mental difficulties, and radiate the energy of goodwill and cooperation for the benefit of the planetary family. And as the energy of *all* relationships, it seeks to prove the truth that there is really only One relationship. Making friends with this angel would seem to be a top priority.

Meditation

God is infinite Love, the great identity in all relationships, the eternal essence of all forms, and this Absolute All-That-Is is my very divine consciousness.

I lift up my mind and heart to be aware, to understand, and to know that the divine Presence I AM is the source, Cause, and quality of every relationship in my life.

I am conscious of the inner Presence as my loving experience of fulfillment, as the harmony in every connection with another being. I am conscious of the constant activity of this mind of total goodwill and joyful unity, therefore my consciousness is filled with the Love of right relations.

Through my consciousness of my God-Self as my source of companionship, friendship, and the quality of every Love experience, I draw into my mind and feeling nature the Light of Spirit. This light is the essence of every bonding with another, thus my consciousness of the Master Self I AM is the cause of every good and perfect relationship.

My inner Light draws to me now those with whom I can relate in love, peace, and joy. Because it is the principle of right relations in action, my desires are beautifully fulfilled, my needs easily met.

The divine consciousness I AM is forever securing the bond of harmlessness and harmony between me and everyone else in my world. Therefore I am totally confident to let God appear as each and every relationship in my life.

When I am aware of my divine consciousness as my total fulfillment, I am totally fulfilled. I am now aware of this truth, and I relax in the knowledge that the activity of divine attraction and right relations is eternally operating in my life. I simply have to be aware of the flow of that creative energy that is continuously radiating from within. I am now aware. I am now in the flow.

(Following the meditation, go into consciousness and make contact with the Angel of Loving Relationships. You know the process and the questions to ask. Listen, and then do your part in the reciprocal relationship.)

EIGHT

The Angel of Victory and Triumph

Edwin Steinbrecher refers to this archetype as "The King in Triumph, Lord of the Triumph of Light, The Conqueror"[1]—and based on my experiences with it I certainly agree. I also look at its function as that of a navigator. This angel takes the goals and objectives that we have received as a vision from our source and guides us along the path of least resistance to reach them, circumventing problems before they arise. If we are blocking those efforts through a fear of failure, a sense of futility in meeting goals, or a feeling of low achievement in life, the bottled-up energy will result in a personality with little compassion or tenderness, one who seems to be indifferent, with no concern for others. In advanced stages it is the energy of the bully, the tyrant.

When I first made contact with this angel, I received an impression that it was the "Energy of Achievement," and when I asked its name, I saw the signature of Serapis. That led to a search through my library for any Serapis references, and I found several in Hall's *The Secret Teachings of All Ages*:[2] "There is . . . a legend which tells that Serapis was a very early king of the Egyptians, to whom they owed the foundation of their philosophical and scientific power. After his death this king was elevated to the estate of a god." He was a key figure in the Egyptian Mystery schools, and it is said that "the neophytes who survived the ordeals were ushered into the presence of Serapis, a noble and awe-inspiring figure illumined by unseen lights." He was also called "the god with the name of seven letters. In their hymns to Serapis the priests chanted the seven vowels."

Significantly, seven is the number of the tarot card representing this angel—the Chariot. According to Alfred Douglas, "Seven is the number of progress, self-expression and independent action." And the divinatory meaning of the Chariot card includes "triumph over the obstacles life throws in one's path . . . victory achieved through personal effort, the triumph of initiative."[3] In another tarot reference we read that "this card signifies the Exalted One who rides in the chariot of creation."[4]

Astrologically this archetype partakes of the energy of Cancer, which represents so much more than many of the attributes generally associated with that astrological sign, such as emotional sensitivity, moodiness, and intolerance. The angels take only the highest aspects of the planetary energies, and the Angel of Victory and Triumph draws forth persistence, boldness, steadfastness, problem solving, powerful imagination, and an understanding of the world of Cause. In radiating the Cancer energy this angel also seeks to fill your consciousness with Light, to illumine you so that you may follow your chosen way with ease and not tread the path in darkness. The key word of this energy is *tenacity*—to help you move toward your goals with determination and resolution.

Could this be the day that you will assume your true identity as the Exalted One, the crowned and victorious warrior riding triumphantly to fulfill your mission on earth? Yes! And the beauty of it all is that you will simply be a witness to the grand accomplishment that will be made in your name. Let's take a closer look at how this angel works as an extension of the great I AM—as the King in Triumph, your total support in victory.

"You will not need to fight in this battle; take your position, stand still, and see the victory of the Lord on your behalf." This instruction from 2 Chronicles 20:17 is one of those coded messages that, once understood, can change your world inside and out. It dramatically describes what happens when you take on the energy of this angel: You literally see the victory before it occurs on the battlefield of life.

Think for a moment about the last stressful, disharmonizing attack that you had in mind and heart. Perhaps it had to do with the breakdown of a relationship, a call to meet a financial obligation when there was not enough money, or something as simple as having too much to do and not enough time to accomplish it all—problems, challenges, aches, and insufficiencies. While they do not exist fourth-dimensionally, they certainly do on the physical-material plane of life, and to pretend otherwise is to ignore the solution. Every problem is a thoughtform, a pulsating energy pattern, a vitalized pocket of mental matter that will continue to exist until broken up and dissipated, which is much easier to do if it is recognized.

Take a moment now and write down three situations in your life that you consider challenges. Set aside any spiritual pride; be honest with yourself and recognize that they do exist and that your life would be happier without them. If you hesitate in doing this, thinking that "this too shall pass" or "I'll handle it in my own way," that's your prerogative. But why not get the difficulty out of the way now and stop waiting for deliverance at some future date? If you say, "My abundance is coming to me," you are really saying that you need money. To think that "this relationship is being healed" means that it is still a mess. To feel that "my health is being restored" implies that you are not healthy. *Now* is the time of salvation, and we must live in the *now* because that is the only place where the problem and solution exist simultaneously.

After you have made a list of your current major problem situations, think for a moment about the positive "mountains" that you want to climb. I am referring to those true ambitions and life goals that reflect the will, vision, and activity of your divine consciousness, yet seem to be almost impossible dreams because of the battles to be fought in time, education, money, contacts, and so on.

Now let's go back to the original instruction: "You will not need to fight in this battle; take your position, stand still, and see the victory of the Lord on your behalf." Look at the challenges and dreams that you put in writing. In order to solve and fulfill them, there may be a firefight on the third-dimensional plane, but you will not need to fight this battle. It is not your fight! So what do you do? You *take your position. Position* in this context means "to assume an attitude in consciousness." It is a frame of mind, a point of view, a demeanor that *it is done, it is finished*, that the problem has already been solved, that the goal has been met on the inner plane. Remember, "before they call, I will answer." By the time you recognized your problem or formulated your true ambition, the solution and the way of success had already been patterned on a deeper-than-conscious level of mind.

How do you bring the pattern into manifestation? First, you must be aware that the divine consciousness, the Thinker-Knower-Doer within, is consciously and constantly *being* all that is or ever will be—all wholeness, all abundance, all success, all relationships, all power, all wisdom, all *All*. After you look at what is happening in your world under the guise of a problem, you turn within and place your attention on that particular attribute of the I AM that represents the solution. With intensity you contemplate the Wholeness I AM, the Abundance I AM, the Success I AM. You "focus the tension" on that which you choose to be consciously aware of being. "I choose to be consciously aware that I am whole and perfect. I choose to be consciously aware that I am infinite abundance individualized." From the standpoint of life goals you would say, "I choose to be consciously aware that the way and the means of fulfilling my divine aspirations have already been etched in my consciousness, and all that I am to do will be revealed as the chain of fulfillment unfolds."

Working from this point of tension—without stress but with a strong pressing in or concentration, and keeping the mind steady on the inherent quality of being and truth of accomplishment—you soon begin to feel the energy of your focus. This is the power of the Angel of Victory and Triumph radiating from the Central Sun within, coming forth as the Energy of Achievement. And now you *are* consciously aware of being that which you desire. "That which I desire, I AM." This is the *have* step in the manifestation process, where the mind and feeling nature shift from a sense of "need" to a sense of "have."

Keep in mind that the energy of this angel will help you feel a sense of victory even before you see the signs and will help you reach your objective by clearing your mind of miscreating thoughts and guiding you through the maze of third-dimensional obstacles.

Think of the attribute of your divine consciousness that you wish expressed and see it as a concentrated mass of energy within. Imagine that this awesome accumulation of Power and force has converged at a point directly behind a thin veil in your consciousness. Your objective is to penetrate that veil and release the Power, and you are going to do this with a laser beam focused in your mind and propelled by your feelings. You work from a point of loving tension to concentrate the beam on the I AM quality (health, abundance, right relations, creativity, success). Using abundance as an example, you contemplate the Abundance of the I AM and let your whole mind and feeling nature be absorbed with the idea of the incredible, inexhaustible, unending, and overflowing supply that is the true nature of the I AM. Let one thought lead to another as you contemplate your true worth as the Spirit of Infinite Plenty.

Soon, in your mind's eye, you will see the veil burning away at the point of concentration, and suddenly your consciousness will be filled with the very Energy of Abundance. From center to circumference it radiates, saturating your being with a realized awareness of itself. This is what it means to "take your position," of being one with that which you wish to be or have.

The next coded instruction is to *stand still*. In the ancient schools "stand still" meant to enter into a state of serenity and trust through complete surrender to the Presence within and to have faith in the activity of Spirit. For a greater understanding of what this means, imagine yourself as a musical instrument, a clarinet for example. See the instrument as you would on a Saturday-morning children's cartoon—alive and animated. It has free will, which means that it thinks it can play itself, so it functions in the world by striking its own keys, blowing its own squealing notes. And all the time the Master Musician is waiting to play the most harmonious melody the world has ever heard.

As time passes, the little clarinet discovers metaphysics and begins to tell the Master Musician within what notes to play for it: "O Mighty Spirit, play the note for a new car for me, for money in the bank and a new job." At first this new way of playing brings results, but they are not lasting. Then the little clarinet seeks to make his demonstrations more "spiritual" and begins to listen for instructions from the Master within as to what notes to play: "Lord, give me the note for health and happiness and I will surely play it in your name." And again some fruit falls from the tree, but the taste is not satisfying. Finally the clarinet's consciousness evolves to the point where it declares, "I surrender to the great I AM THAT I AM. Master, play your notes through me!"

How does the instrument make the transition from attempting to play itself to where it is finally used by the Master Musician? Through contemplative meditation on the Truth of Self. We give up our sense of need because needs are based on experiences of the past, and the God-Self works in the now. We do not tell the Self what notes to play for our fulfillment because it already knows. And we do not ask the Presence to tell us what notes to play because we simply are not accomplished Master Musicians. We let the Presence of Self come into our consciousness and play the notes from its level, and the music is so different from ours that we are awestruck. And through the new song played by the Master we could well find ourselves experiencing dramatic and positive changes in life—a relocation, a new career, a completely new way of living—because the Master will be playing its own tune of master fulfillment in and through and as us.

Through this standing still the "victory of the Lord" is accomplished, just as the divine Presence through its mighty angels triumphs over every less-than-divine condition in your world. The I AM Abundance charges out "to do battle" with lack and limitation; the I AM Wholeness moves through your body to eliminate imperfection; the I AM Success goes before you to blow away obstacles. All that is left for you to do now is "see the victory." Can you in your divine imaging faculty capture the picture of completion? If not, lift up your vision. It is done, it is finished. See it! The Law of Victory and Triumph works through right attitudes in consciousness, a surrender of the lower nature, and a vision of fulfillment. It is a law that never fails.

The Angel of Victory and Triumph is the perfect example of the principle of Victory in the mind of God. Victory, as a universal law, constitutes Reality without opposition, which means that defeat, failure, and loss are illusions with no substance or power to support them. This original pattern of triumph and supremacy was given to all souls as a Causal Power, an aspect of God, to lead us through the difficulties of life.

Remember that God has given the angels "charge of you to guard you in all your ways" (Psalm 91:11). As with the other angels, this Agent of Cosmic Law works *naturally* to fulfill its purpose if its energy is not blocked by ego projections. When we consciously work with it, we rise safely above the troubled waters. For example, a friend who worked regularly with the angels managed to overcome a fear of crossing a mile-long bridge over a lake, a trip that she has to take twice a week. She said, "I have a tremendous fear of water and in the past have had to stop the car before getting on the bridge because I was shaking and my heart was pounding so much that I couldn't drive. With the help of the Angel of Victory and Triumph the fear is conquered. 'Tis done!' sang the angel."

Now think about the times in your life when a feeling of tenacity rose up in you, when you persevered against all odds and emerged victoriously as the conqueror of limited conditions and restricted situations. Whether you knew it or not, this angel's powerful energy was obviously working in and through your consciousness to strengthen your determination and to shed light on your path, and now you can see that this is in order with the natural process, a part of our essential nature.

For a major part of her life my mother has charged through fields of despair and turmoil with sword in hand, meeting every seeming impossibility without a thought of defeat. Whether starting a business from scratch to provide for the family during the Depression, losing everything and beginning anew, enduring a severe illness, or rebuilding a life after the deaths of my father and stepfather, she prevailed and found a new joy in living as she moved through with each experience. Because she has great compassion in her heart, high self-esteem, and little fear of failure, she has been able unconsciously to tap into the Victory energy and overcome obstacles that most people would consider too formidable.

Taking a page from her book—and before I had an understanding of the Agents of Power that are available to all of us—I jumped a hurdle of my own and was able to fulfill the dream of my life. In high school and college I ran track, and although I had my share of ribbons, I was only in the fair-to-good category. Later, while in the air force and stationed in Germany, I came home for a forty-day leave in December 1952 and "discovered" Jan. We fell madly in love, and when I left to return to Germany, my only thought was that someday we would be married.

Upon my return to the air base in January, I noticed a bulletin posted in squadron headquarters inviting those interested to try out for the base track team. The last paragraph caught my eye. It detailed the various meets that were scheduled throughout Europe, culminating in the All-Europe Games and stating that the winners of each event would be taken to the United States in June for the Worldwide Air Force Track and Field Meet. Suddenly I realized that this was my opportunity to get back home and marry Jan.

Terribly out of shape and in competition with men who had been stars at major universities in the United States, I began the training program for the 110-meter and 400-meter hurdles, never losing sight of my ultimate objective. Obviously the appropriate angel took charge, and in crisscrossing Europe over the next four months I did not lose a race and set new air force records in the high hurdles. When we arrived in New York in June, I called Jan, proposed over the phone, and three weeks later we were married. She later flew to Germany and we began a life together that has been greater and grander than I could ever have imagined. Truly, nothing is impossible when the Angel of Victory and Triumph is riding on your shoulder.

I am sure that you can recount numerous stories of men and women who have fought the good battle and won—including yourself. And if you have tasted victory even without a conscious awareness of this angel, think what you can do when the two of you work together as friends and teammates. Remember that the Angel of Victory and Triumph is the Energy of Achievement, the Power to be, the Light that shines through barriers, and the force of the victorious warrior. Let him fight the battle for you. Your role in the scheme of things is to know that you have already won, to trust the divine process, and to see yourself crossing the finish line with arms held high. Your angel will help you to do this with ease and grace, so take the time following the meditation to move up in your force field and make contact with him. He's just waiting to go to work on your behalf.

Meditation

Beginning now I will live in the now, for only in the now are the solutions to life's problems found.

(Contemplate what it means to "live in the now.")

As I look at my world, I take notice of anything that is less than ideal from the standpoint of my present state of consciousness. This need not be, and so I call forth the divine remedy.

First, I forgive myself and others for all miscreations and I absolve myself and others of all guilt from the past. I am now ready for victory in every undesirable condition and to triumph over every disharmonious situation, and I call on the Angel of Victory and Triumph to fill my consciousness with its energy. I feel it! And to the angel I say, "In preparation for my personal encounter with you I release all fear of failure, all sense of futility, and all feelings of low achievement in life. I see only victory in all that I do, and I see everyone everywhere achieving their soul's purpose for the good of all."

I now turn within to behold the Exalted One I AM, omnipotence in action, and I perceive in this glorious divine mind the answer to every question, the solution to every problem. As I contemplate the divine qualities of the I AM THAT I AM, I feel these gifts of God enter my awareness. All that I could ever seek, I AM, and all that I AM is now expressing in perfect form and experience.

I now have total fulfillment in life. I have taken my position, and I stand still in quiet serenity and perfect trust, beholding the victory of the Lord and Master Self I AM. It is done. It is finished. I AM Victory.

(Now proceed through the corridor of consciousness to meet, love, and appreciate this Causal Power of the Victorious Self.)

NINE

The Angel of Order and Harmony

During meditation one morning I began pondering the idea of a fourth-dimensional person living on the physical plane and how he or she would appear to others. And soon a composite profile emerged, perhaps based on the common denominators of all the illumined ones that I had read about or had met personally. And the sum total or completed picture seemed to portray the aura and essence of what I would call divine order.

There was the perfect balance between head and heart, will and love, inner and outer, work and play, stillness and action, impression and expression, listening and speaking, receiving and giving, radiation and attraction. This imaginary person in my vision surely knew how to live! There was an easy, relaxed energy field and a consciousness of total equilibrium, which is another word for stability—defined as steadiness, soundness, and poise. Everything seemed to fit together, which is the meaning of the Greek work *harmozein*, the origin of our word *harmony*. And a by-product of this order, balance, and harmony was peace, a radiation of serenity and tranquillity.

How wonderful it would be if we all expressed this kind of energy, this state of consciousness. Our self-image would certainly be different, and without fear and guilt we might even begin honestly to like ourselves. And it goes without saying that people would greatly enjoy being in our presence. But we cannot fake it. I know from personal experience that if we try to play the role of total order and harmony for very long from the angle of the human personality, we become nauseatingly nice robots, overly controlled sweet-machines with a patronizing air that turns everyone off. Haven't you known people who presented a surface perfection so thin that you could see right through it? And behind the mask of flawless superiority was a churning mass of suppressed fear and anger.

To truly *be* order and harmony, you must take on the Energy of the Soul that produces such qualities, and then you *are*—and no role playing is necessary. You may be surprised to know that the energy manifesting as these attributes is *joy*. Order and harmony are born out of joy, and not the other way around. The Angel of Order and Harmony is the "joy of the

Lord," the Master Self's pure energy of exultation, ecstasy, and jubilation that radiates like the midday sun to remove the shadows of sorrow, misery, and despair. And it does this by establishing balance and stability in life.

Show me someone who lives in the radiance of joy and I will show you a person who "fits together" with the world like hand and glove, where everything is in sync and functioning as a harmonious whole. I'll give you an example to explain what I mean.

Several years ago I realized the profound impact that joy had in my immediate environment by experiencing the lack of it. I did not know that I was "joyless" until I sought the answer to a ridiculous turn of events where everything seemed to be out of kilter. During a very specific time frame the car broke down, the lawn mower fell apart, the clothes dryer died, the TV went on the blink, and my business affairs gave the appearance of a soap opera. When I finally stopped long enough to go within and ask, "Why me?" I heard the answer: "Your joy vibration is practically nonexistent, and joy is the energy and the catalyst for order and harmony. Without joy all forms held in consciousness begin to disintegrate, for joy is the energy of fusion and unity."

This was quite a revelation for me. Then I was led to read John 15:1–11 again, where Christ spoke through Jesus in the message of the True Vine: "I am the vine, you are the branches . . . he who abides in me, and I in him, he it is that bears much fruit, for apart from me you can do nothing . . . these things I have spoken to you that my *joy* may be in you, and that your *joy* may be full" (italics mine).

We see from this Scripture that the joy in individual consciousness does not come from outside, but from the Master Self within, the I AM, and that this joy is made full through the act of abiding in that Presence. What does *abide* mean? It means to stay with, live, reside, dwell. When we are consciously aware of the Presence of the divine consciousness, which means that we have realized that it is *present*, we become in tune with the Energy of Joy because the song of the soul is joy! The vibration of the omnipotent I AM is pure joy, and when we catch that vibration, we bear much fruit—not only in attracting new good to us but also in correcting and protecting the good that is already manifest in our lives.

It did not take long for me to go within and touch the hem of joy and abide there for a time—and when I did, the Angel of Order and Harmony must have been released from the chains of ego because the strangest things began to happen. I intuitively saw what was wrong with the lawn mower and had it running in no time. The car, which had sounded like a cement mixer and would run for only minutes at a time, healed itself. When the repairman arrived to fix the TV set, he couldn't find anything wrong with it; it was picture perfect. Meanwhile, back at the office, we landed two new clients, received payment on several past-due bills, and our productivity jumped to a new level. Oh, yes, the clothes dryer. As I said, it died, but it later reincarnated as a brand-new one. I guess the angel decided to do that rather than replay the Lazarus story.

Later I spent considerable time researching the idea of joy and how it affected order and harmony. I found that what we call happiness comes from the personality and is constantly subject to the winds of change blowing in an individual's world. But joy comes from the divine consciousness of the I AM and infuses the personality with its energy when the mind is consciously anchored in the higher realm. Joy opens the curtains of mind and lets in the Light, and the darkness is no more. *A Course in Miracles* says, "The world you see does nothing. . . . It merely represents your thoughts. And it will change entirely as you elect to change your mind, and choose the joy of God as what you really want. Your Self is radiant in this holy joy, unchanged, unchanging and unchangeable, forever and forever. . . . Lay down your arms, and come without defense into the quiet place where Heaven's peace holds all things still at last. . . . Here does the joy of God belong to you . . . joy alone is truth."[1]

The twin flame to joy is serenity, and once the fire of joy and serenity dominates the personality, all outer conditions are controlled in the Light, which explains how joy literally creates and maintains order and harmony in our lives. First of all, *the greater the joy, the greater the flow of energy.* As Dr. Douglas Baker put it, "In that aspect of consciousness which we call joy . . . energy inflow is at its greatest, in the sense that such energy is the most easily transformed into outward activity through the personality."[2] Secondly we should understand that joy is a Power that controls the lines of force that govern electrons and cause the appropriate clustering of atoms in a natural order. When joy is withdrawn, the atomic structure of matter is altered, resulting in disorder and disharmony. As I have said, we can use the personality to pretend to be joyous, but even the greatest acting ability will not delay the eventual outer deterioration caused by weakened lines of force, which can affect all physical expression, from the body to the bank account.

I should also point out that an individual expressing true joy from the Kingdom within does not run around trying to make everybody happy, and neither is he or she the life of the party. A joy-infused consciousness is more like a beacon of calm in a storm, a light of ecstasy dispelling the darkness. A joy-filled person is in rhythm with the universe—warm, contented, peaceful, balanced, poised, and confident, with a jubilant heart and overflowing with gratitude. And the outer reflects the inner, with everything "fitting together" in perfect order and harmony.

Isn't it time to start singing the song of joy? Let the Magnificent I AM teach you the words and music—with invaluable assistance from a very special Causal Power, the Angel of Order and Harmony.

This angel is feminine in nature and stands at the vortex between the causal realm of divine consciousness and the personality. In the Greek Mystery schools she was called Athena. In addition to her other powers and functions she was considered the goddess of the arts, and the city of Athens was named after her. The Romans called her Minerva, and thought of her as the goddess of war—as evidenced by the sculpture of her in the Vatican Museum, which shows her wearing a helmet.

How can an angel associated with war be considered the Angel of Order and Harmony? Because divine order, the first law of the universe, can only be achieved through the destruction of that which is in disorder. Bringing this down to the level of the personality, we can see that an ego-desire for harmony may cause you to compromise your spiritual integrity as you give in and accept a negative situation "for the sake of" agreement and amiability, but that kind of thinking will not transmute the disharmony. The ego says, "Don't express your truth or inner knowing, just go along with the insanity in the name of peace." However, peace at any price is not the way of this angel. She's a warrior in angelic attire and she will not accept chaos, confusion, and turmoil. She doesn't think twice about blowing away these problems in a very positive and powerful way. "When Christ said that He does not come to bring peace but a sword, He proclaimed a great truth. No one can have peace until he reaches a state of balance, a state of equilibrium, in which his spiritual progress is not hindered by any physical, emotional, mental, personal or social problems."[3]

It is also interesting to see what happens when this angel's power is blocked. When we screen her out with lower-nature feelings of sorrow and despair, the ego attempts to borrow her sword and imitate her warrior stance by sending messages on the desirability of conflict—the idea that attack is justified for self-protection. The personality becomes an antagonist and a creator of further disorder. Without ego projections on her she will maintain the natural flow of the joy energy as it moves into manifestation as order and harmony in our lives. She does this through inspiration—motivating us to selfless service for the joy of it, to maintain balance and fairness in all situations, and to live with integrity. She works with the form-building energy of all manifestation, seeking to transmute negative circumstances and to maintain the lines of force at their most harmonious level.

Mythology tells us that when Greece was weakened by war and chaos, Athena produced the olive to bring order and stability to the land. In the early 1970s, when Jan and I were going through a period of severe business upheaval that seemed like a battleground, Athena produced a dog. She was an English springer spaniel, and we named her Lady Brandywine of Yorkshire, or Brandy for short. This gift of the angel immediately took our minds off our problems, brought balance into our lives through joy and gratitude, and saw to it that things moved up to a more harmonious state in all our affairs. When she made her transition ten years later, she quickly returned as Magnificent Brandy Too (Maggi for short)—and the amazing events of her "reincarnation story" are detailed in my book *Practical Spirituality*.[4] She came back at one of the most crucial periods in our lives, a time of a complete change in my career, which involved the founding of the Quartus Foundation and the publication of my first book, *The Superbeings*.[5] And she has been with us every step of the way as a "beacon of calm" and a "light of ecstasy."

Angel Athena produced something else for me on July 14, 1985. I had been reviewing the draft of chapter one in *Practical Spirituality*, where I discussed the mass and velocity of the negative energy at play in the world and the hope that we can change that mass from rocks to feathers. During a brief moment of concern I was shown very graphically that the Light will indeed prevail—when a gray, three-inch feather suddenly materialized in my study. Talk about tears of *joy*! This angel works in mysterious ways to keep us in the harmony of balance, to inspire us with trust in the future, and to keep us moving on higher and higher spirals of life.

In the tarot this angel is symbolized as Justice—a crowned figure carrying in her right hand a sword and in her left a pair of scales. This card "teaches that only balanced forces can endure and that eternal Justice destroys with the sword that which is unbalanced."[6]

The word *balance* comes from the Latin phrase *libra bilanx*, which is significant since the Angel of Order and Harmony utilizes the particular energy of Libra as a quality of divine force. This energy deals with choices, choosing the way through a careful weighing of values and achieving the right equilibrium between the pairs of opposites to find true harmony. John Jocelyn says, "When this harmony is won by overcoming the fierce onslaught of inner conflict and by suffering trials in the flesh, the riot of desires finally having been brought under full control, then do we behold a man filled with true compassion for humanity. Libra evokes a passion for peace and brings peace through passion, for in this sign harmony is achieved through conflict."[7]

Through the Libran energy this angel works to inspire the individual to world service and converts inertia into a dynamic force for the achievement of divine justice in the world. I have no doubt that this angel played an important role in stimulating Jan and me to develop the plans for the first World Healing Day on December 31, 1986. It was in September 1983, while on a flight from Alabama, that I heard the words "World service! It is time!" This led to the writing of *The Planetary Commission*[8] and the announcement on January 1, 1984, of the simultaneous global mind-link to be held at noon Greenwich time on the last day of 1986. The *Los Angeles Times* said, "It was billed as the biggest participatory event in history" and quoted the figure of "150 million to 400 million" participants. Based on computer analysis of information from sources worldwide, the number actually exceeded 500 million, and the numbers have grown each year.

We can almost see the angel working powerfully through this bonding for healing and peace to achieve a new balance in world affairs. With helmet on head and sword in hand she went forth to transmute disorder and reveal harmony—if necessary, through conflict. In January 1992 I received a letter from a man in the Pentagon: "A New World has literally come into being. All over the planet seemingly invincible dictatorships have fallen, and the spirit of freedom and democracy has taken root in nearly every land. I believe that spiritual historians of the future will mark the date, December 31, 1986, as a turning point in history."

Remember that each of the twenty-two angels has a cosmic duty to emit the true nature of its being to help you in the awakening process. They are divine thoughtforms with divine intentions, but they are subject to the energy that we are consciously or unconsciously radiating, which means that we can change their nature and paralyze their expression. The Angel of Order and Harmony is particularly vulnerable to our overpowerment because the collective consciousness is conflict-oriented with a vibration tend-ing toward disorder. So we must be constantly alert and take immediate action to cancel out states of mind appearing as selfishness, judgment, criticism, intellectual pride, coldness, and narrowness.

We counter these shortcomings through the energy and power of joy—the joy of the Lord I AM—and we let the feeling of joy be our natural state of being. Then the angel is freed—and the first law of the universe—divine order—becomes the dominant factor in our lives.

Meditation

I quiet my mind and still my emotions and go within to the secret place, and I sense the overshadowing of the great I AM THAT I AM, and I move into the glorious Light of the Kingdom consciousness.

The kingdom of God is my very own divine mind, my I AM God consciousness, where everything is complete, finished, and in perfect expression. The divine ideas of all that is invisible and visible are right where I AM. The angels of the Kingdom are right where I AM. There is nothing but perfect fulfillment in the Kingdom I AM.

I am in the Kingdom now, for I am aware of the Truth and the fullness of my being. I am in the Kingdom now because I AM the Kingdom, and all that God is I AM, and all that God has is mine. And among the treasures of God I AM and have is the energy of pure joy.

I let the song of joy begin in my mind and heart as I accept this divine attribute. It is mine because it is what I AM, and I consent this day to abide in the glorious Self I AM so that the eternal joy may be in me and my joy may be full.

I feel the joy flowing through me now and I partake of its essence: great serenity, peace, Light, warmth, contentment, poise, confidence, and a jubilant heart overflowing with gratitude. And my joy goes before me to create and maintain perfect order and harmony in my life and world.

Now, in the name of the Holy Spirit of God, I call forth the Presence of the Angel of Order and Harmony. Her Light appears before me, and with deep feelings of love and thankfulness I say to this holy helper, "I pledge this day to remove the burdens that I have imposed upon you, and I free you to do your perfect work according to the highest vision of the great I AM." And the angel speaks, and I listen.

I am now abiding in the presence of joy, and joy is now the natural state of my being. And I let order and harmony reign supreme in my life. I choose to live in perfect peace with honor and integrity, and I am ready to fulfill my role as a dynamic force for the achievement of divine justice in this world.

This is the moment of my new beginning. I now move forward with great joy to do that which is mine to do.

TEN

The Angel of Discernment

The mystics of the East considered this angel the Archetype of Karmic Deliverance. Among the Gnostics of early Christianity it was the power of grace, the energy that removes the error stains of past misdeeds from consciousness and helps us to control our destiny through the quality of discernment. This of course relates specifically to the Law of Cause and Effect. In previous chapters we only touched on this law, so now let's give it our full attention as the major determining factor of life on the third-dimensional plane.

Cause and effect, action and reaction, compensation, and karma—which all mean the same thing—were taught as part of the "natural sciences" in the sacred academies of the ancient past. The students were told that through specific actions, effects are produced, results become manifest, and that by being consciously aware of the law they could use it to escape the victim vibration and improve successive states of existence.

In truth there really is no such thing as "bad" and "good" karma. It is simply a natural force to enable an individual, a group, or a nation to reap what is sown. The ancients considered it the plan of eternal justice where payment in full is demanded for past indiscretions, yet it was also taught that if the law was rightly wielded, it would produce great happiness—a chain of fulfilling consequences, joy, and freedom.

The ancient schools with their "pagan" rituals seem so divorced from today's Christianity that one may find it difficult to believe that Jesus taught basically the same course of instruction. Knowing that karma means that every act is followed by some kind of result—that is, an action produces a reaction—we can look in the Bible and find the ideal description of this natural process. It's in Luke 6:37–38: "Judge not, and you will not be judged; condemn not, and you will not be condemned; forgive, and you will be forgiven; give and it shall be given to you; good measure, pressed down, shaken together, running over, will be put into your lap. For the measure you give will be the measure you get back."

And in Luke 8:17–18 we see how consciousness becomes its own karmic force: "For nothing is hid that shall not be made manifest, nor anything secret that shall not be known and come to light. Take heed then how you hear; for to him who has will more be given, and from him who has not, even what he thinks that he has will be taken away." And Paul stated in Romans 2:1, "Therefore you have no excuse, O man, whosoever you are, when you judge another; for in passing judgment upon him you condemn yourself, because you, the judge, are doing the very same things."

Just as in the Mystery schools, Jesus and Paul were teaching the effects of causes emanating from consciousness, but they were also providing lessons from Ageless Wisdom on the *art of discernment*, particularly as it relates to being prudent and judicious with impressions made on the great "cosmic recorder and playback machine." With a multitude of examples and analogies we are told how to lay a proper foundation in consciousness to avoid karmic repercussions and are admonished to *think* before taking a specific action, with the consequences of the act carefully explained.

Moses wrote very clearly about the law of compensation in Deuteronomy: "life for life, eye for eye, tooth for tooth, hand for hand, foot for foot." While the literal meaning is usually emphasized, Moses was an initiate in the Mysteries and surely meant this to be interpreted symbolically. Then hundreds of years later Jesus affirmed this direct-line cause-and-effect relationship showing that we get back the very same nature that we give. Paul's line about the person not having any excuse was just a way of saying that karmic law does not make allowances for ignorance.

This teaching was a way of establishing guidelines for living successfully on earth, for when we were born, we entered a force field that is both extremely dangerous and highly beneficial. We came into a karmic vibration that accepts every thought, word, and deed and plays it back to us in an interconnected life experience. Every mental, emotional, and physical action triggers a chain of causation, a ripple effect that moves toward infinity—with each ripple sending back a reaction to the originating individual, continuing until the effect of the cause is resolved.

This force is a part of the natural order of things and is to be respected but not feared. We must simply learn to work with it, and for those of us on the wheel of rebirth, we will continue our physical life cycles until every cause resulting in a violation of the principle of good-for-all has been canceled. Ralph Waldo Emerson wrote,

> Is not the law of compensation perfect? It holds as far as we can see. Different gifts to different individuals, but with a mortgage of responsibility on every one. "The gods *sell* all things." The whole of what we know is a system of compensations. Ever since I was a boy I have wished to write a discourse on Compensation; for it seemed to me when very young that on this subject life was ahead of theology and the people knew more than the preachers taught.
>
> Polarity, or action and reaction, we meet in every part of nature; in darkness and light; in heat and cold; in the ebb and flow of waters; in male and female. . . . Superinduce magnetism at one end of a needle, the opposite magnetism

takes place at the other end. If the south attracts, the north repels. To empty here, you must condense there. The same dualism underlies the nature and condition of man. Every excess causes a defect; every defect an excess. Every sweet hath its sour; every evil its good.

Thus the universe is alive. All things are moral. That soul which within us is a sentiment, outside of us is a law. We feel its inspiration; but there in history we can see its fatal strength. . . . The dice of God are always loaded. Every secret is told, every crime is punished, every virtue is rewarded, every wrong redressed, in silence and certainty. What we call retribution is the universal necessity by which the whole appears wherever a part appears.[1]

Since the thoughts, words, and deeds that affect "compensations" are based on what we believe, it would only seem prudent to check our belief system—comparing what we actually believe with what we *think* we believe. The truth is, we really do not know what we believe until we see the effects in the outer world. We say that we believe in harmony, goodwill, and right relations, but perhaps we are more certain of a hostile world, a competitive jungle, and obstructive forces. It is the latter that will be impressed on the sensitive karmic plates, producing personal conflict, opposition, and bondage—and all this will continue until the beliefs are changed.

The same principle applies to every other activity of life. Do you believe more in wholeness or illness, abundance or scarcity, success or failure? What you believe, you are, and whatever you are conscious of being impresses the karmic field to bring you the fruits of your consciousness. Let's begin now to work *with* the Law of Cause and Effect rather than against it. All it takes is discipline and dedication to learn the ancient art of discernment. To be discerning means to be perceptive, astute, discriminating, judicious. It means to be constantly aware of your thoughts, words, and deeds and to think, speak, and act only from the standpoint of *harmlessness*. It means to be sensitive and shrewd in the examination and restructuring of your beliefs in order to ensure that they are based on the Truth of Being and not on appearances.

We pay off the karmic debt registered in the body by eliminating irritation and hostility and by transmuting our anger into a purposeful intention to live in wholeness. Instead of fighting the disease, we begin building a consciousness of health by letting our conscious awareness dwell on the wholeness of the perfect Master Self, and we stay with it until the realization experience occurs. We practice preventive medicine by living with Unconditional Love to impress only will-for-good on the karmic field. We stamp "paid in full" on the karmic obligations in our finances by moving above a sense of futility in life and by correcting the sense of separation from our source. We cease the struggle against insufficiency and concentrate more on understanding that our consciousness of the abundantly rich I AM within *is* our supply. We are what we are conscious of being!

We look at every area of our lives and we go to work to produce a chain of fulfilling consequences stretching out into infinity. We have it all and we have it now, and *now* is the time to make certain that the universal karmic nature receives this impression with all of the force of our divine consciousness. And fortunately we have a holy helper who is ready and able to act on this intention.

In some Mystery schools this angel was called Adonis. By the Egyptian and Persian priestcraft he was considered one of the world saviors who was crucified and rose again. When initiated into the Mysteries of Adonis the neophyte passed through the death of sin (missing the mark through the lack of discernment) and into a state of redemption, with Adonis himself paying the karmic penalties.

Little is known of the process of initiation except that renunciation was a major part—a formal giving up of all the claims of the senses and a rejection of appearances. Much time was devoted to periods of seclusions to discover "correspondences" (causes and effect), followed by instructions in the "knowledge of being separate from the root of opposing forces." It is interesting that the root word of *discernment* comes from a Latin term meaning "to know enough to keep separate."

Those who fulfilled the requirements were committed to be members of a secret organization for life and to shield the secrets of the Mysteries from the adulteration of the masses. The graduates of the Adonis School took with them the knowledge of a spiritual power within, a quality of divine force that we are calling the Angel of Discernment.

According to Greek mythology, "Adonis was a handsome youth. . . .

Aphrodite (called Venus in Roman legend) fell in love with him. She warned him against the dangers of hunting, but he paid no attention and was killed by a wild boar. Aphrodite in her grief changed his blood into a flower which is called the anemone, or windflower. Proserpina restored him to life, but he had to spend six months of the year with her in the Lower World. The other six months he could spend with Aphrodite. This myth helped to explain the rebirth of nature in the spring."[2]

Many times we, too, have intuitively felt that a particular action was not in our best interests, yet we shrugged off the admonition and later paid for our failure to listen by "dying" of embarrassment, regret, failure, and deprivation. Ignoring what we know to be true guidance for right action does produce a corresponding effect. Adonis was brought to life by the "Underground Queen" but had to fulfill his karmic obligation by living with her underground for six months each year. Sound familiar? Even when it appears that we've been mortally wounded through our transgressions of the law, life goes on—and until the slate is wiped clean, it may seem that we are living in hell half the time. I know.

My objective as chief executive officer for an advertising and public relations firm in Houston was to attract top creative talent and make our company nationally known as one of the "hot shops." A man from England heard about us and applied for the position of creative director. His credentials were impeccable, and with his British accent and dashing appearance he seemed to fit our every requirement. Working for me at the time was a "goddess of the treasury"—our comptroller and head of the accounting department. After speaking briefly with Mr. Whiz, she said to me in confidence, "He's bad news. If you hire him, you'll later regret it." Something inside of me echoed her sentiments, but I threw caution to the wind, and two weeks later the "James Bond" of the advertising world was on our payroll.

He made quite a splash at first, which made me feel that I had done the right thing—and I reminded everyone of my genius in choosing all the bright stars for our team. But before six months had elapsed, he had conned me personally out of a large sum of money and had fled the country. Talk about dying. Seasons in the abode of the damned became quite normal as I went through many peaks and valleys and feasts and famines with the company. But payback time wasn't over. I later hired a salesman for a client of mine and against my better judgment loaned him some money until his first check came in. He cashed the check and left town.

Over the years I finally learned discernment and in the process overcame a tendency to play the victim through self-pride, indiscretion, and impetuous action. When I began the study of the angels, I realized that I had blocked the energy of this Causal Power through a consciousness focused almost entirely on the effects of this world rather than the Cause, as well as a strong desire to separate myself from people because of uncertainties in dealing with them. In the cases mentioned above, "separateness" was certainly evident when the two men beat a path out of town after taking advantage of the vulnerability that I was projecting.

I later found that this angel will work through our intuition to keep us on the straight-and-narrow path of high perception and deep discrimination. He will train our consciousness to judge rightly and enable us to work in the realm of Cause to realize fulfillment, peace, and freedom. Through the energy of this angel we will know the proper door to open and the right action to take in the ultimate mastery of karmic forces.

In the tarot this angel is represented by the Hermit and portrays an aged man denoting judiciousness, prudence, and circumspection—a seeker after truth, a pilgrim on the path to enlightenment. "He personifies the Wise Old Man, the teacher who points out the thread of meaning that is woven into the apparent chaos of life. He illuminates the primeval darkness with the light of higher consciousness, and drives away the shadows of the night."[3]

Astrologically this angel is represented by the energy of Virgo, symbolizing the valley of silence and deep experiences. The angel works with this energy to remove barriers that are blocking the realization of the Christ principle and to impress us with the idea of subordinating the material world to the Will of God, thus lifting consciousness above the retribution aspects of karma. The Virgo energy is the latent Christ Consciousness, and the seed that leads to the fruit of this consciousness is the idea of divinity in the form—the unity of spirit and matter—"Christ in you the hope of glory." Virgo is the energy that helps us overcome a condemnation of the material world as nonspiritual, and through it the Angel of Discernment teaches tolerance, compassion, and charity as the way of karmic control.

In *Watchers of the Seven Spheres* this angel tells us that he is a symbol "of divine prescience—of thought without emotion"—and that he strives "ever for unity, harmonizing the conflicting vibrations . . . to transmute the errors and the fears, the conflicts and confusions which arise through man's own blindness, into ultimate benefit, bringing swift retribution that he may learn to associate Cause and Effect and recognize that evil and destruction breed nought but dissolution, and love and harmony alone will lead him toward the Perfect State."[4]

You may want to read this message again and then consent to accepting the angel's assistance in harmonizing your conflicting vibrations and removing your blindness to the Law of Cause and Effect. It may require additional periods of solitude because he works most effectively in the silence to condition consciousness to be more prudent and judicious. In the quietness of your mind he will help you to see the Truth and to carry it with you to discern the rightness of every situation in the busy world around you. Then there will be only one season, a perpetual time of harvesting the fruit of the good seed.

Meditation

In the quietness of my mind I am consciously aware of the Presence of God I AM, and I contemplate my Holy Name: I AM . . . I AM . . . I AM . . . I AM . . . I AM . . . I AM . . . I AM.

In the stillness of my Holy Self I am conscious of the watching, listening, sensitive nature of the cosmic field of causation all around me. It is receiving even now the pulsations of my mental and emotional energies. It hears every thought, feels every emotion, responds to every word, reacts to every action.

I seek to impress upon it only that which is good, true, and beautiful, for that is how I see my life and my world from the divine perspective. I know that I am not alone in working with this great, receptive, Causal Force.

Within the magnificent radiance I AM stands the Angel of Discernment, my guide to high perception and deep inner knowing. Come forth, my angel. Let the Holy Spirit lead you into my awareness now.

I feel your Presence and know that you are now free to be the Light of holy discrimination in my consciousness. And I commit this day to thinking, feeling, speaking, and acting only for the highest good of all.

Now is the time of my new beginning. I am a cocreator with God, and it is a new heaven that comes as the goodwill of God is expressed on earth through me. It is the Kingdom of Light, Love, Peace, and Understanding, and I am doing my part to reveal its Reality.

I begin with me. I am a living soul, and the Presence of God dwells in me, as Me. I and the Father are one, and all that the Father has is mine. In Truth I am the Spirit of God.

What is true of me is true of everyone, for God is all, and all is God. I see only the Spirit of God in every soul. And to every man, woman, and child on earth I say, I love you, for you are me. You are my Holy Self.

I now open my heart and let the pure essence of Unconditional Love pour out. I see it as a golden light radiating from the center of my being, and I feel its divine vibration in and through me, above and below me.

I am one with the Light. I am filled with the Light. I am illumined by the Light. I am the Light of the world.

And my life is good, so very good.

ELEVEN

The Angel of Cycles and Solutions

The waiter brought the bill and the plate with four fortune cookies. I selected one, cracked it open, and pulled out the slip of paper. It read, "Hitch your wagon to a star." That phrase was originally coined by Emerson, my philosophical hero, so I mentally connected my earthbound system to my fourth-dimensional radiance and sat back to enjoy the image. Then the thought ran through my mind of how words on a little piece of paper can boost our confidence and conjure up scenes of happiness and fulfillment for us.

The amazing thing is that we express such glee over an effect hidden in a hollow Chinese pastry when we have the Cause of fortune right within us, the Master Self who is expressing as all good fortune at every moment in time and space. That is our Truth, but until we reach that remembered state of consciousness, we find ourselves enduring the ebb and flow of "cycles" as aspirants, disciples, and initiates. The old mystics said that life was the "journey of the wheel." For those anchored in the lower nature I have called it the roller-coaster ride of delight and despair. The writer in the Old Testament (Ecclesiastes 3:1–9) called it "seasons"—a time for everything including killing, mourning, hating, and warring.

Regardless of what the traditional religious teaching has said about the ups and downs of life, I agree with the mystics and sages of the past who taught that the only place we can go is up, that the spiral of life is always in the ascendancy. For those on the spiritual path I like to think of it as an escalator ride, and while the moving stairway may curl around the mountain, the motion is always to a higher level. Yes, there are cycles and cyclic forces and rhythmic processes, but they are divinely designed to propel us forward. The tale about the "Fall" under the apple tree has etched such a lie in consciousness that we are always looking down or back over our shoulders to see when misfortune might catch us. That's what false programming can do.

Now, you are probably wondering why you appear to be caught in the briars of the ravine when the law says that "up, up, and away" is the Truth of life. The two primary reasons usually are: (a) You have been *unaware* that the spiral will take you from one expansion in consciousness to another, and then another, until you reach the mountaintop of illumination; without the awareness of this governing principle and the way it works, the mandate simply does not apply; and (b) You have guilt over some imagined wrong action on your part that you feel, unconsciously perhaps, deserves some form of punishment. By accepting the omnipresent Energy of Divine Forgiveness that is constantly pressing in on consciousness, and by forgiving everyone including yourself for the past, you will transmute the guilt and suspend the sentence.

Just remember that you have never made a mistake in your eternal life. What you did at the time was consciousness-in-action, and you really had no choice but to do what you did because that is where you were in consciousness. The Law of Consciousness always outpictures itself, and it was perfectly fulfilled through your actions in thought, word, and deed. Therefore your actions were perfect—regardless of the karmic obligations incurred.

Let's take a still-closer look at the cycles of life. Your divine consciousness, the Reality of you, has its own beat, vibration, and rhythm. By adjusting your mind and feeling nature to your own particular soul pulsation through meditating, listening, and living the spiritual life, you can rise above the hill-and-valley experiences. There will continue to be periods of intense activity followed by interludes of going within in order to assimilate the divine impressions, but you will soon move beyond the sense of duality with its highs and lows of health and sickness, abundance and lack, harmony and conflict, joy and sorrow.

Look at the example of a spiral shown here and draw an extended version on a separate piece of paper. In reality it is a coil of pure energy that begins in the lowest animal nature of the individual and moves up to the higher triad of the God-Self. Right at this moment your conscious awareness of Truth exists as a point of Light somewhere on that spiral of energy—perhaps in the lower quadrant, or near the middle, or even approaching the curls at the top.

Notice that the line of the spiral is moving up, then begins to level out and fall back but catches itself in time and gets back on track. It then resumes its upward arc to form a new pattern and continues the coiling process in rhythmic harmony. This is what life looks like in a mystical sense, and each new "coil" is an initiation or expansion in consciousness. When we become synchronized with this life design by identifying with it, we find ourselves in the universal flow and in tune with the cyclic impulses and energy rhythms.

The problem for most of us is that we focus our attention almost exclusively on the objective world—on the world of Effects—and forget that our life purpose is to concentrate on the upward spiral of consciousness, which is Cause. When we enter into periods of seeming inactivity in life, which we may think of as seasons of dryness, and feel that we are accomplishing nothing, let's remember that the energy spiral is simply lowering its rate of vibration in order to move into a new and higher level of activity. I recounted in *The Superbeings* that an awakened one told me that "any experience of contraction is a gathering of power, power which will flow according to the clearest picture that we hold in mind."[1]

What this means is that even when our lives seem to be restricted, there is no reason to be concerned—and in particular we must not let the fearful horror movies of "what might happen" play in our mind. We are to remember the spiral and know that the Power is gathering force for a mighty leap into a new activity of increased good, and we use our creative imagination ("the clearest picture") to see only joyful fulfillment in every area of our lives. And during those times of intense outer activity just know that the pulsation of the soul has increased to reveal a new cycle of experience and growth, sometimes a strenuous endeavor of building and developing to greatly enhance the quality of life.

When wholeness, prosperity, and harmony are outpictured, we know that we are in the rhythm of Spirit and are being carried into even greater degrees of heavenly experiences. But when the form side of life flags our attention with signs of illness, insufficiency, and conflict, it means that we have temporarily left the energy curve—our life design—and are floundering around in the empty space off the spiral path.

The Angel of Cycles and Solutions will help us get back on track. In the old schools this angel was known as Jupiter (Zeus in the Greek Mysteries) and was thought of as the personification of cyclic law, the Causal Power of expansion, and the angel of miracles. Unless blocked by ego projections of thoughts such as "this is too good to be true," "this good can't last," "I just know that something bad is going to happen," this angel will help you to stay firmly on the path regardless of what is going on in your world. And it frequently does this by prompting a change of attitude, enabling you to feel your way back into the energy stream, reconnect mentally with the Master within, and remember that you are on a journey in consciousness. He will inspire you to surrender again to that indwelling Presence and let the omnipotent Cause be in charge of the cycles in your life—and will impress upon you the inner knowing that each upward curl expands consciousness, reveals the solution to problems experienced in the curve below, and brings you closer to your ultimate perfection.

In the sacred academies the Angel of Cycles and Solutions that was discovered in our psyches was called Jupiter in honor of his standing in mythology as controller of fate and the power to bring good into individual lives. This energy of poise, confidence, and the belief in a positive future will permit you to accept change without fear and move into each expansive cycle with greater self-assurance and boldness. Remember that change is part of the natural order of things, which means that switches in jobs, shifts in careers, geographical moves, group reorganizations, restyling of family life, altering of partnerships, and so on are the result of cyclic impulses. These changes should be accepted with the attitude that you are on the spiritual spiral of life with absolutely nothing to fear.

In early 1982 I knew that my life was about to change dramatically, but I could not get any clear direction regarding what I was supposed to do as a cocreator in the transformation process. Even though we had established the Quartus Foundation, Jan and I were still running our own businesses. We were also busy filling the orders for *The Superbeings* that were coming in daily, and our workday frequently extended far into the night. I kept asking for guidance, and it finally came in a dream. An old man, whom I now believe to be the Angel of Cycles and Solutions, took me to the top of what he called the tallest building in the world and told me to jump. I peered over the edge and became very frightened and said, "It's too far down. I'm afraid." And he said, "You must take the step." With those words he put his arm around my shoulder, and we stepped off together. I found myself floating like a feather—no panic or struggle, only great ease, peace, and a sense of freedom. The next morning Jan and I agreed to close down our business operations and devote our lives to spiritual research and communications—to writing books and providing service to others as best we could. Jupiter had given us the solution for moving successfully into the next cycle: "Take the first step and leave the rest to me." And when we did, resulting in the removal of the major channel for our income, the needed supply was quickly provided through calls to give lectures and workshops.

At the beginning of another cycle this angel led us through a major change and a truly expansive stage, including a move from Austin to Boerne, a small town northwest of San Antonio. There was not one moment of pressure or concern as we and the entire Quartus staff joyously packed up and headed for new horizons. Offices were provided on Walter Starcke's Guadalupe River Ranch, and we all found perfect living accommodations within a matter of hours. In August 1987 we began holding workshops on the ranch, including an annual Mystery school.

Jupiter also alerts us when the spiral is in a lower rate of vibration and we have not properly prepared for the upcoming new pattern of life. He once appeared before Jan in Roman clothes with a wreath on his head, saying, "Nero fiddled while Rome was burning. As for you, I can only expand what you give me to expand." He then changed his appearance and became the head and upper body of a centaur, which symbolizes aspiration and ambition. Jan felt that he was telling her to stop frittering away time, that she was ignoring an important opportunity during this period to examine and contemplate certain personal and business activities that would be highlighted in the next upward spiral. Finally he said, "Focus your thoughts on what you really want in life." Through this "lesson" she was able to rearrange her priorities, dispense with certain activities that were not productive, firm up her aspirations, and prepare herself for the coming expansion.

In a very real sense the Angel of Cycles and Solutions takes us by the hand and gently leads us on the curving path, meeting the challenges and solving the problems of the previous cycle at each intersecting point of the upward arc. These solutions are revealed by showing us with great clarity that the problem never existed in the first place, that it was a miscreation in mind. When the problem's energy was withdrawn, the appearance of the problem vanished. If this energy is screened out by an overactive ego, we become egotistical, vain, and pompous, and we mask our fear of the future through arrogance. Our life continues on that roller-coaster ride with over-emphasis on "security" and the status quo.

A visitation I had with this angel in December 1991 revealed why many people are afraid of the future. Here are excerpts from my journal:

> During their visits to Planet Earth people construct a particular dwelling place in consciousness. In that place they have a name, a body, and a buildup of overlapping experiences which they call life. Their motto is Make the best of it, meaning that they must learn how to live with the cards they have been dealt, to be as happy as possible during their stay in a strange land. They develop zones of comfort, contentment, security, and certain expectations—all boxes where they feel at home. But the universe does not know about boxes. The Self cannot be confined to finite space. Its stretch is infinite and its Self-fulfillment cannot be denied, and that

is why it admonishes all not to be possessed by possessions, not to concretize their lives, to stay open and be prepared and ready for change, for change is its very nature, and it will have its way no matter what. The personality must consent to go along for the ride—to be flexible, moldable, and to follow the way of the Self that leads through the maze. The I AM leads the way to the future by the lamp of Truth, which reflects the true meaning of life, and that is the significance of the biblical verse of "I AM the way, the truth, and the life." All souls must reach the juncture where they are willing at a moment's notice to sell all, uproot themselves from all that is known and comfortable, say good-bye to family and friends, and move toward the new horizon—even if they cannot see it at the time. But I can, and I will help all to follow the Light.

In the tarot this power is symbolized by the Wheel of Fortune, a card that signifies happiness, opportunity, expansion, and solutions to problems. It portrays a wheel with eight spokes, the Buddhist symbol of the Cycle of Necessity.

From an astrological perspective this angel utilizes the energy of Jupiter in its work of transformation. This energy is on the love-wisdom ray and seeks to develop and bring into synthetic interplay the individual's head and heart, mind and love, and will and wisdom. It is the ruler of expansion,

the conveyor of miracles, and it is said that all who work consciously with
the energy of Jupiter are also in tune with the Law of Supply.

Pause for a few moments now and make contact with this mighty angel.
Let Fortune be your guide as you circle the mountain in your upward climb
to mastery.

Meditation

*The Angel of Cycles and Solutions is my holy helper, my guide on the
pathway to illumination. In my oneness with the Spirit of God I AM, I see
change as the natural order of things, as the breathing in and breathing out
in the divine process of manifestation. Without hesitation I fully accept
change in my life, knowing that only my highest good is expressed in every
upward cycle.*

*I stand at the vantage point of the eternal now, poised in peace and power
and beholding only God at work. I feel the uplifting action of the omnipotent Presence within and know that my life is expanding, my consciousness
evolving, my good multiplying.*

*As I journey up the spiral of life, I know that the activity of my Master Self
is the perfect Law of Harmony and Divine Order and that there is nothing to fear. The divine consciousness I AM goes before me to prepare*

the way and remains with me as my shield of protection, and I am not afraid.

I now release all inhibitions, all insecurities, and all uncertainties, and I move ahead with faith and boldness to accomplish that which is mine to do. I now go forth with uplifted vision into my ever-expanding universe.

I pronounce my life good, so very good!

TWELVE

The Angel of Spiritual Strength and Will

What happens when an irresistible force meets an immovable object? Nothing, if you happen to be both the force and the object, which you are on the higher side of life. Suppose someone attacks you with criticism. Should you respond in kind? No, and neither do you fret over the verbal assault. You stand in the Light of the Master Self you are and know that the superpower within is your strength and shield.

Regardless of the "news" that we are given on any given day—termination on the job, the announcement of the end of a relationship, the loss of our fortune, a pronouncement by a doctor—we must learn to handle such revelations with the attitude that "none of these things move me." We become the immovable object that then radiates the irresistible force to dramatically transform the intimidation, the threat, the verdict.

Shakespeare wrote, "Cowards die many times before their deaths; the valiant never taste of death but once." How many times have we "died" in our lifetime? A loss of power and resulting meltdown occurred because we were not "valiant"—not courageous, undaunted, bold, daring, and fearless—the very attributes that release the cold, clear fire of the Energy of Transmutation into the phenomenal world. This is the energy that remolds and recasts every situation and condition into a divine scenario for the good of all concerned.

Where do we find this Power and how do we become one with the irresistible force and immovable object? By removing the block that we have imposed on the Angel of Spiritual Strength and Will. I am not talking about being strong enough to "cope" with a situation or possessing a wimpish will that says, "I'll make it through somehow." I am referring to a Causal Power so potent and mighty that it can literally dematerialize a so-called threatening situation and reveal the reality of the divine standard standing firm beyond the shadows.

I have written about the poisonous activity of criticism—both in word and in thought—and its destructive action, but perhaps I have not sufficiently emphasized the fact that the one who suffers the most is the criticizer, not the one who is criticized. This is particularly so if the latter is on the spiritual path. To me a critical mind is a cowardly mind because the root of criticism is resentment, which can be traced to wounded pride and on down to the seed of fear—an ego-fear of rejection.

It is interesting that the negative traits of an individual whose ego has blocked the Angel of Spiritual Strength and Will include a defiant, disrespectful personality. And the block is usually caused by spiritual weakness—a lack of commitment to the spiritual way of life and a belief that the world of form offers greater pleasure than the inner world of Spirit.

Criticizers are not the only ones with a seal on this power center. Consider anyone who "falls apart" in a so-called crisis, or who accepts the negative judgments and conclusions of others, or who constantly vacillates with no clear purpose and seems always to be caught in the struggles of life. These states of consciousness are also working out of the lower nature with little or no conscious awareness of this natural force within. Then we look at the other side of the coin and recognize those who have tapped into this power.

Several years ago a friend of mine was told that her condition was inoperable, that there was no hope. This was totally unacceptable to her, and she told the doctor in no uncertain terms where he could stuff the diagnosis. Then she went home and got well. A man I worked for, a vice president of a large corporation, came to his office one morning and found that he had been fired. His files had been cleaned out and his personal effects were in boxes on his desk. He was stunned, but instead of lashing out at the president he centered himself and remembered the old axiom, Whenever one door closes, another quickly opens. Within twenty-four hours he was offered a position with another company at a sizable increase in salary.

There are countless other stories of men and women who "stood in steadfastness" while the storm raged and found that every adversity had a seed of a greater benefit: A business failure led to right livelihood in a new career; a divorce enabled a couple to find their true partners in a new and joyous, loving relationship; the death of a loved one brought forth an initiation into cosmic consciousness for the one left behind. Each case history revealed quiet strength, great courage, strong emotional control, and the complete audacity to trust God regardless of the seeming appearance.

None of this is new to those of you who have studied the wisdom teachings and the Bible—that codebook for mastery. In the ancient schools the initiates were taught the power to dare by facing formidable struggles and, through the power of strength and will, to slay the dragons of self-creation. Then they were led to the final battle—the task of tracking the lion of the personality into the cave and mastering it, emerging as a sun god and world savior.

A quick review of the Bible reveals many passages about the Energy of Strength and Will, including that incredibly powerful message in Philippians 4:13: "I can do all things through Christ which strengtheneth me." Ponder that statement and feel its power.

Through the *feeling* of strength (firmness, fortitude, backbone) comes the *knowing* of will (purpose, determination, resolution)—and this fusion of heart and mind is the action of an awesome energy flowing from the supermind within through a vortex of divine force controlled by an arche-type of cosmic law. This is the Angel of Spiritual Strength and Will.

This living energy has been called the Daughter of the Flaming Sword, implying a feminine quality. However, this angel is a synthesis of both feminine and masculine energies, since the aspects of strength and will are perfectly blended into one power or force. The wisdom teachings tell us that strength in itself is passive, whereas will is active. Yet strength provides the force to give power to will. So we must consider these qualities as one when working with this angel, knowing that out of the poise and quiet of strength (the daughter) comes the activity of will (the flaming sword).

In my contacts with her she has appeared as a young woman with magnificent might. Her pulsating light body seemed analogous to a sleek, high-powered automobile standing ready for acceleration with a rhythmic revving of its engine. I felt that if her force were unleashed, I would be filled with such an infusion of energy that even an earth-shattering event would not cause an emotional ripple. Fortunately I did not have to undergo such extreme experiences to appreciate her fortitude and determination. When I consented to be on a radio call-in show in 1985 to discuss the first World Healing Day and the global mind-link for peace scheduled for December 31, 1986, I was not prepared for the venom that poured from the mouths of many of the listeners. Jan and I were called followers of Satan and tools of Lucifer, and when I invited all religious faiths to pray together on that day, one man called us the anti-Christ and threatened us with bodily harm. Enter the Angel of Spiritual Strength and Will. As the hostility grew stronger, so did the energy emanating from this Causal Power. I felt my consciousness growing in firmness and vitality, enabling me to speak my Truth without fear or rancor. From that day forward our determination to do whatever was necessary to assist in the transformation of this world was raised to a new high.

I should have had a clue to the power of this energy when I saw my friend Sako, a small Japanese man, defend himself from an attack from two large thugs. They were throwing a barrage of insults, and I knew that they would soon be using their fists. Suddenly the little man stood up, closed his eyes for a second, then opened them and stared intently at each antagonist. Neither of them spoke. They began to back away, and when they reached the door, they turned and quickly left. I turned to Sako and asked what he had done. His answer: "If I can see myself clearly as unlimited power and unconquerable, so can others who are riding their emotions. I did, and they saw."

I can remember a time when Jan was having great difficulty letting go of a dilemma that was causing a mental and emotional disturbance. She came into my study and asked me to meditate with her, and within a few minutes she tapped into the energy of this angel. Jan said, "I felt a tremendous surge of energy move into my back and heard the words, 'I am the strength of Jehovah, mighty in battle to slay those who would defile me.' I knew then that I could call on that strength to slay those things in my mind that were dishonoring my Reality, and I did so. The emotions quickly became still waters, my mind became clear, and I knew that the challenge was over. Not only had the angel slain the miscreations in mind, but she had also won the battle in the manifest world as the troubling situation vanished and perfect harmony was soon revealed."

When I fell off of a high wall one night at a friend's house and rolled down a steep hill, I knew that something had broken, but I also realized that no one could hear me and that I needed help. I called on the angel, and in a matter of seconds I could feel that "rhythmic revving" taking place in my energy field, giving me the strength and will to climb that hill and get assistance. I made it without too much difficulty, and when I was told later in the emergency room that I had a broken pelvis and hip, I gratefully acknowledged the Daughter of the Flaming Sword for being the "hand of the Lord" in that anxiety-provoking situation.

Let's contemplate the word *will* for a moment. We all talk about free will and God's will without realizing that they are one and the same. Our free will is our free use of God's will, which is concentrated in our divine consciousness. This means that our intuitive guidance, our true aspirations, and our loving intentions all represent the will of our Master Self—and to accept anything less than the highest and greatest in life is to deny that will.

The tarot symbolism tells us more about this angel. The young woman in this major trump represents spiritual strength, and the picture shows her hands on the mouth of a lion. The lion here is symbolic of the one mentioned in 1 Peter 5:8 ("your adversary the devil, as a roaring lion, walketh about, seeking whom he may devour"). This is a direct reference to the ego-dominated personality, which must be controlled and mastered before the advent of the Christ Consciousness. This card also implies liberation, achievement gained at considerable risk, and a capacity for accomplishment.

In astrology this energy is represented by Leo, and the Angel of Spiritual Strength and Will draws on the Leo energy to provide the aspirant with enthusiasm, inspiration, confidence, and vitality. She also works in consciousness to tame the lion of aggression, overconfidence, and self-satisfaction. As we open to this angelic energy, our personality gives way to individuality, and "from the cave" a new person emerges—the Lion of Christ. There is now the spirit of universality, with the radiating power of emotional determination, mental will, and physical fortitude directed for the good of all.

John Jocelyn has written, "The Lion . . . is the symbol for strength, the strength that pulses throughout the world, making all things possible of fulfillment and surging through the world as creative power. Strength, power, and will are the attributes of this kingly sign, Leo."[1] In *The Symphony of the Zodiac*, Torkom Saraydarian says, "Leo is 'the birthplace of the individual' who is equipped by the will-to-achieve with strong self-determination."[2]

Here are some excerpts from my journal relating to the teachings from the Angel of Spiritual Strength and Will, which revealed to me a new depth of understanding of this Causal Power. I shall not attempt to reinterpret these words to provide greater clarity and understanding. I will let you do that, and in the process, learn more than I could ever give you with my paraphrasing.

"Why do you seek a power from the without? Is it to overcome another power which you perceive as an effect and are resisting? An effect in your life is merely a creation of your mind, which may appear to threaten you. And human nature is to resist that which threatens, yet whatever you resist you give energy to, and whatever you give energy to continues to live. Why not remove the obstacle to your peace by withdrawing its power? You do this by knowing that the only power in the universe is within you, not outside of you, therefore anything you see in your world has power only by your decree. Break the decree and the order is countermanded, and the intimidation vanishes.

"You have believed in the instruction to 'take your position, stand still, and see the victory of the Lord'—yet you often fail to call on me to strengthen your stand. I am an anchor in shifting waters, the guyline in a storm, and I will hold you firm in your non-resistance and steady in the Light of the one Power that is shining in your world.

"You need not pray for deliverance from the adders, or for the harmonizing of any situation in life, for to do so is to deny the Love, Wisdom, Will, and Power of God that is eternally in full performance through you. The only true prayer is one of gratitude for that which already is.

"This situation that is disturbing you, think on it for a moment. Know that it can be resolved for the highest good of all as you are strong in the Lord and understand that your challenge is of no concern to God. To be 'strong in the Lord' is to be impassioned toward Self, intensely devoted to the One within with only will-for-good, seeking nothing for the personal self. I will give you this strength, this will, and this selflessness, which together releases the Higher Power from any obligation to perform specifically for you. Then the Self can be about the Father's business without any interference from you. And what is that business? It is the business of being Itself, of fulfilling Itself for the glory of the Father. How does It fulfill Itself? By radiating all that God is to the world. Now, in order to reach the world, that Radiance must pass through the consciousness of personality. If one is strong in the Lord, consciousness will translate that Radiance into whatever is needed, and what is perceived as the solution to the problem is revealed. The spark of Truth in consciousness does this; in illumined ones it is a flame. This Fire of Truth in consciousness is the watchman of Isaiah and Jeremiah, the one at the Gate that interprets the invisible flow into visible experience—to substantiate the Truth of Being.

"Do you see what you must do? You must cease looking to a Higher Power to renew your world because it is not your world; it belongs to Self and Self is maintaining it for Itself as heaven on earth. As you let go of your world of mind and become strong in the Lord, the Truth frees you of anything that is less than Truth. You then live without difficulties and challenges because you are no longer living in your world . . . you have entered the Fourth Dimension."

Become aware of this living energy, this agent of divine manifestation. Make contact with her and understand her nature. Know and be one with her quiet, poised strength, and take up her flaming sword as the divine will-for-good. Become the irresistible force and the immovable object—the power to dare with fearlessness in the doing. As J. Sig Paulson, a Unity minister, lecturer, and author of several metaphysical books, has written, "Rejoice in the growing strength of your own inner selfhood. Stand tall in the stronghold of your own integrity. More and more you will be able to stand in peace, the strength of soul that moves you from being a 'fighting' element to being a 'lighting' element in the world."[3]

Meditation

Quietly, gently, easily, I turn within and become receptive to the Light and Love of my Holy Self. With the inner eye I see the Light flooding and saturating my entire energy field, and I feel the Love filling me to overflowing.

I am in Christ and Christ is in me, and there is no separation, for there is only the one Light, one Self, one Presence—the Presence of Love. And out of this master mind of Light and Love flows the invincible, omnipotent, all-consuming fire of strength and will.

It is my strength, my will, and I accept this divine energy of courage, firmness, fortitude, purpose, determination, and resolution . . . totally, completely, fully. I dare to do and be because I know who I AM.

And to the Angel of Spiritual Strength and Will, I pledge to you a new commitment to the spiritual way of life and to harmlessness in thought, word, and deed. I choose to tame the lion of personality and emerge from the cave as the Lion of Christ in service to this world. And I listen now as you reveal to me that which I must do to help you in your magnificent work of creating and sustaining my divine Reality.

(Listen)

I am now strong in the mightiness of Spirit and I am undaunted. My mind is firmly one-pointed in seeing only the good. My heart is fearless and knows only the emotion of victory. Nothing can touch me but the direct action of God, and God is my omnipotent Self in radiant expression. I can do all things through the strength and will of the Christ I AM.

THIRTEEN

The Angel of Renunciation and Regeneration

Renunciation means "a giving up, letting go, surrender." *Regeneration* is defined as "being reborn into Spirit; restored to original state of being." Accordingly, to awaken to our true identity, we have to give up something, often at a sacrifice. But once we break out of the dream, we see that it was not a sacrifice at all, only a replacing of the lesser with the greater.

From the time of the first sacred academies and the restoration of the Mysteries, right up through the writing of the New Testament and continuing with the teachings of the secret societies of the seventeenth and eighteenth centuries, the first principle in the Awakening process was renunciation. It was the platform for spiritual rebirth and the foundation for Selfhood. It is such a critical course of action that not a single Mystery school, religion, esoteric teaching, or spiritual philosophy omitted it from their traditional disciplines. And every spiritual master on record has considered this "giving up" process the prelude to mastery.

In *Codex Rosae Crucis*, a rare Rosicrucian manuscript dated between 1775 and 1780, we find a plate that reads in part, "I know nothing, I want nothing, I can do nothing, I love nothing, I glory in nothing, I delight in nothing, I seek nothing, I also wish for nothing in heaven and on earth except the Living Word alone."[1] This "Living Word" refers to the one essential divine Self of each individual—the Logos, Christ, Word of God. When nothing else matters but the realization of this divine identity, we are going through the renunciation initiation.

The Tibetan master Djwhal Khul says that "to hold, one must detach, and to keep, one must release. Such is the Law. Life, for the disciple, becomes then a series of detaching processes, until he has learned the lesson of renunciation."[2] This early teaching from Ageless Wisdom and later echoed by Paul was based on the truth that *when you have nothing, you possess everything*. This is the guiding principle of the Angel of Renunciation and Regeneration, and as I have written, "This must be our creed if we are to gain our freedom and be all that we were created to be. I, John, cannot bring peace to this world, and neither can I feed the multitudes, heal the sick, harmonize relationships, or prosper those in the bondage of debt and limitation. No, I can't—but the Holy Master Self Who is the Reality of each one of us can."[3] We begin by giving up our mortal sense of existence—by detaching ourselves from what we consider the "personality" and becoming identified with the Master Self within, our divine consciousness. In this process of changing identities we surrender all that has been acquired by the personality. We give up the entire inventory of the lower nature to the higher because the higher cannot infuse the lower until the lower is empty of all that it was. The lesser must be sacrificed for the greater, otherwise the spiritual rebirth cannot occur. Where do we begin? Consider this list of twenty personality characteristics:

1. The tendency to criticize
2. The tendency to assume the responsibility for others that is not yours to assume
3. The tendency to surrender to someone else the responsibility for your own welfare
4. A feeling of needing to be cared for and protected by another person, which relates to point 3 above
5. Spiritual pride and the tendency to prove your spirituality by giving unsought advice or spiritual "counseling"
6. Selfish personal ambition
7. Personal self-pity
8. Sensed personal power
9. A sense of futility

10. The tendency to find relief and release through alcohol or drugs

11. The tendency to play a "misery loves company" game

12. Emotionally controlled relationships of any kind, including those with spouses, children, parents, and friends

13. Deception and dishonesty

14. Fear and guilt

15. Feelings of unworthiness

16. Identification with the body as the Self and a preoccupation with the physical form and its needs

17. An emphasis on personal security

18. A feeling that "my truth is higher than your truth," that "my mission is grander than yours"

19. A Messiah complex

20. A spiritless consciousness—no vitality, fire, light, animation—living without inspiration

The Great Renunciation, the final step before Regeneration, takes place after you have recognized every personality characteristic and complex, focused on each one, disengaged it from consciousness by casting it upon the Holy Fire within, and worked daily to live without this adulterated energy. It takes discipline, but with every detachment more of the Light of Self moves into the personality. Coming up from the dark cellar of the lower nature is not always a smooth, upward glide; it can be a tough and strenuous climb. But remember, you are not in incarnation just to put bread on the table, pay the rent, plan for your security in later life—or to be a help-less jellyfish or a threatening shark. The sacred literature and the silent voices say one thing: You are here to be reborn in Spirit, and then to share that blazing infilling Light for the benefit of the world.

When this is your motivating intention, something strange and wonder-ful takes place in the mundane affairs of life. You begin the process of loving detachment—and with every release something better takes its place. And soon you will notice that practicing harmlessness is natural, that giving others their freedom to fully experience life is fulfilling for all concerned, and that you, too, can be truly independent with no concern for security. You will find that you do not have to prove anything to anyone, and the self-pity, futility, fear, and guilt will be gone along with the need to escape. You will rise above the hypnotic pull of the third dimension as you realize that you are the Kingdom of pure energy, and with that understanding, lack and limitation will only be fading memories of the past.

The entire process of renunciation and regeneration is summed up in my book *A Spiritual Philosophy for the New World* in what I call the sixty-day Non-Human Program.[4] The idea is to devote sixty days to breaking the ego connection by surrendering every mental, emotional, and physical pull—releasing everything that has bound you to the wheel of struggle and strife—and then to move into the energies and vibrations of the fourth dimension, not as a human being but as a spiritual being of Light. For the hundreds of men and women who participated in the initial experiment in 1988, the sixty days became a lifetime commitment. And while I do not mention the Angel of Renunciation and Regeneration in that book, he was greatly instrumental in showing me that breaking the ego connection does not mean treating the physical world as nonspiritual. Rather, it is to balance the absolute with the relative and see the unity of spirit and matter through the single eye of divine consciousness. It is living as a spiritual being in physical form.

Let's meet the Angel of Renunciation and Regeneration. Remember that this is not some sort of winged fairy floating in your energy field or a creature imagined in the mind of a Mystery-school master eons ago. These angels are living forces and conscious energies in the causal body, functioning as whirlpools of Power. In their natural-order process they extend the vision, activity, and Creative Power of the divine Self into personal consciousness as a ray of light. And the light of this particular angel is to maintain consciousness in "the surrender mode"—to help us relinquish all sense of separateness with the master soul and to prepare the personality for the "Great Infusion of the Lord." If that energy is blocked through the ego's projection of fear of loss and deprivation, we develop a victim consciousness, a suspicious and jealous nature, and a feeling of being everyone's prey.

In many of the ancient schools this angel was known as both Neptune and Poseidon. In Greek mythology, Zeus, who ruled the earth, gave Poseidon all the water of the earth. Poseidon was the brother of Zeus, and when we view this relationship in terms of the angels, we see that good fortune and a positive future are directly associated with a cleansing of the old and becoming "a new creature" in the heavenly Self within. According to the *Metaphysical Bible Dictionary, water* is defined as that which "breaks up and dissolves old error states of consciousness in the individual, just as the Flood dissolved and washed away from the race the old conditions that the combined error force of individuals had formed."[5] So we see that even in the myth stage, Poseidon (god of the waters) can be associated with renunciation as he directs the dissolution of the error patterns that we have released to its energy.

When the initiators in the Mystery schools took the name of Poseidon, they based their teachings on the transformation of human nature, a dying of the personal sense of self and rebirth into spiritual consciousness. The initiates were asked to bring to mind the attributes of their true sacred identity, the ideal Self, and then to compare their lower natures with the higher. Every property of individual being that did not measure up to that Holy Image was to be sacrificed and crucified on the cross symbolizing the Angel of Renunciation and Regeneration.

This angel has appeared to my inner vision as a large older man, seeming to express both great compassion and strength in his expression. I tuned into him one day when I was trying to surrender a situation for the highest good of all, and he asked me, "Are you willing to have all outer forms washed away?"

And I said, "I would be lying if I answered in the affirmative. I really don't want to dissolve the 'thing' itself; I just want to release it for divine adjustment, along with the feelings that are pulling on me."

"Until you are willing to let it go completely, it cannot be rebirthed. And the feelings you speak of, are they not your feelings of how others will feel if you remove something from their lives upon which they seem to be dependent?"

I said, "I never want to take any action that will affect others in a less-than-positive way."

"Then decide otherwise, and let the action truly be for the good of all. You know that the manifest form and activity that you speak of is only a projection from your consciousness, and if you believe that it is necessary for your happiness and the happiness of others, you are once again removing God from your life—and from theirs, in your perception. Be amenable to my energy; be *willing* to surrender everything and then do so. Release, release, release! Think not that you must rely on, protect, or nourish an effect of mind for your good or for the good of others. Dependence on anything in the phenomenal world must be broken."

I said, "Out of feelings of love for others, we sometimes get confused as to the proper course of action. I guess that from an overview, caring too much can be a hindrance."

"Personality ties must be detached in order for there to be a bonding on a higher level, for love from one ego to another is only a form of prison for both. In truth, the only responsibility you have is to yourself; to assume responsibility for another is limiting for all."

"Is surrender my only alternative in this situation?" I asked.

"What would you do if someone called you and asked for prayers in a similar circumstance? Or for help in meeting *any* challenge? You would not for one moment, concentrate on the person or the problem, because there is absolutely nothing you could do! You could not fix bodies, make people prosperous, mend a relationship, or find employment for some-one—regardless of how hard you prayed. No one could because prayer was not designed to do those things. Instead you would immediately turn within to the one Presence and Power—not to ask anything of God but consciously to be in oneness with God in an attitude of total surrender. And in that oneness comes deliverance for all as the Truth of God is demonstrated. The person, or persons, will receive their release in accordance with where they are in consciousness, and with what they are choosing to experience. But it is no longer your concern, for the creative activity of Spirit is now in charge."

He then appeared much larger in my field of vision and said, "Loose everything and let everything go. Empty yourself of all responsibility toward anyone, of all obligations to others, of all feelings that you must solve another's problems. Release the world that you have made with mind and just *be* . . . just *be in God*. You will find new life, and those who are reaching out to you will find that there is only one source of salvation, and they will grow mightily with this realization."

Following that encounter with the angel I felt freer than at any time in my life, for I finally understood what is meant by "I of myself can do nothing."

In the tarot symbolism this angel is shown as the Hanged Man, signifying sacrifice, surrender, renunciation, resurrection, and regeneration. In referring to this major trump, Manly Hall says, "To attain the heights of philosophy . . . man must reverse (or invert) the order of his life. He then loses his sense of personal possession because he renounces the rule of gold in favor of the golden rule."[6] In *Highlights of Tarot*, Dr. Paul Foster Case tells us that the primary meaning of this card is Reversal. "This refers to the reversal of thought, a point of view held by those who know from that held by the unenlightened multitude."[7]

In esoteric astrology this angel corresponds to Neptune, known esoterically as the Initiator. Dan Oldenburg, a professional astrologer, wrote an article in *Planet Earth* magazine about the planet Neptune. Here are a few significant excerpts in which he clarifies some words associated with it:

> One is: compassion. But compassion should never be something like "duty." That is false. Let existence choose. My experience has shown that if "I" choose, there are going to be problems. Because I don't know. Existence reveals the unknown to me. . . . Another word associated with Neptune is surrender. Surrender, to me, doesn't mean giving up my freedom. Surrender means allowing existence to come in. How else can there be any real freedom unless I surrender to the whole? This is the essence of Neptune—surrendering, dissolving, melting, merging, drowning. Surrender is the thing. It's a non-method method.[8]

It is through the energy of Neptune that the individual takes the Second Initiation in Ageless Wisdom—the purification of the lower nature as symbolized by the baptism of Jesus. This is the initiation that moves the individual from personality consciousness to Christ Consciousness and the beginning of true service to the world. Isn't it time to fully participate in your baptism? This is the washing away of everything that binds you to humanhood and allows the Spirit of wholeness to descend and infuse the lower nature, and you begin to live the attributes of the Master Self. Remember the principle of this angel: "Have nothing and you possess everything."

Meditation

Into the dynamic energy vortex of the Angel of Renunciation and Regeneration I release everything that has bound me to the wheel of struggle and strife. To the angel I say, "I willingly sacrifice the lesser to realize the greater, and I hold nothing back. I seek to be clear and clean in preparation for the divine infusion, and I ask you, What can I do to help you fulfill the renunciation and regeneration experience in my life?"

(Listen)

This is the day that I cease identifying with my personality and judging the personalities of others as virtuous or dishonorable. From this moment on my conscious awareness will be directed to the Holy Self I AM as the only Reality of my being, as the only Reality of everyone. In truth there is neither man nor woman; I AM is the pure energy of God in individual expression.

And to this Presence of God I AM I say, "I accept your Light, Life, Love. I let your Mind be my mind, your Thoughts my thoughts, your Vision my vision, your Power my power. I seek nothing in this world, only God's glorious expression through me."

I am in the Silence now, and I see that nothing but God exists. I AM THAT I AM . . . the one Light, one Life, one Love. And I behold the Mind of that One, and the Thoughts, and the Vision, and the Power. I AM that ONE.

I rest now in the Experience.

FOURTEEN

The Angel of Death and Rebirth

The force of this angel is an extension and amplification of the flow of the Causal Power of Renunciation and Regeneration discussed in the previous chapter. It is as if the Angel of Renunciation and Regeneration yields the next class instruction to the Angel of Death and Rebirth to complete the lesson of replacing the lesser with the greater. Alfred Douglas says that this archetypal energy "continues the story of the Hanged Man."[1] According to Dr. Paul Foster Case, it "does not represent the end, but the real meaning of Death . . . the gateway to a larger life in reality."[2] So consider the work with this angel as the next grade in the course of spiritual rebirth.

This angel represents the force of metamorphosis, and its function is to help us dissolve the error patterns and false beliefs of the ego and condition our consciousness for the final infusion of the God-Self energy. It is "that irresistible impulse in Nature which causes every being to be ultimately absorbed into the divine condition in which it existed before the illusionary universe had been manifested."[3] If this energy is blocked because of the fear of the ego's "death" and the diminishing of the personality, or through the identification of the physical body as the Self, we will be resistant to change and will block the divine spontaneity of life. Negative ego projections can also result in a constant monitoring of the physical body to see what is wrong, leading to disorder in the system.

This divine agent was symbolized in Greek mythology as Thanatos, the god of death. To the Romans he was Mors: Their Greek and Roman brothers were Hypnos and Somnus, respectively, the gods of sleep. Since the ancients believed in immortality and a continuance of life beyond the veil, their view of death as being related to sleep can be seen as a direct reference to the majority of humankind who live in a state of slumber in physical form, unaware of the Reality of being.

The name of Thanatos was also carried into the early Greek Mystery schools, but in most of the academies this divine force was known as the Master of Death. The Initiator who assumed this role tested the students as they passed through the death of the personality, awakened them to Truth, and they were reborn as the divine Self. This angel is also symbolic of the Eighth Labor of Hercules, the destruction of the Lernaean Hydra.

Hercules was told to do battle with the loathsome beast with nine heads, and according to Dr. Francis Merchant in *The Labours of Hercules*, the Teacher said to Hercules: "One word of counsel only I may give. . . . We rise by kneeling; we conquer by surrendering; we gain by giving up."[4] When Hercules encountered the beast, he swung his club and lopped off one of its heads, but two quickly grew in its place. As the battle proceeded in the water and mud, the monster grew stronger. Then, according to Dr. Merchant, "Hercules remembered that his Teacher had said, 'we rise by kneeling.' Casting aside his club, Hercules knelt, grasped the hydra with his bare hands, and raised it aloft. Suspended in mid-air, its strength diminished. On his knees, then, he held the hydra high above him, that purifying air and light might have their due effect. The monster, strong in darkness and in sloughy mud, soon lost its power when the rays of the sun and the touch of the wind fell on it. . . . Fainter and fainter grew its struggles till the victory was won."

While we may not think of our ego as a nine-headed hydra living in "a stench-drenched bog," this animal nature does represent the accumulation of all unconquered personality defects from all our many incarnations in physical form. In the myth Hercules ("the son of God who was also the son of man") is symbolic of the aspirations of one on the path of discipleship, a seeker after Truth who will do what needs to be done to reach the ultimate goal of Selfhood. Notice that when attacked with a weapon (symbolic of anger and fear), the beast replaced and multiplied its severed parts, and as Hercules continued to fight in the bog, the hydra grew stronger. This tells us that if we set upon the ego with warring emotions, we are only magnifying its malevolent nature, and by fighting on its territory—in the murk of lower consciousness—our power to overcome is dissipated. In dealing with this lesser and unredeemed part of our nature we must remember that "we rise by kneeling"—indicating that humility is the key, with pride and anger replaced with patience and forgiveness. So we cast aside our hostility and raise this self-created thoughtform into the purifying light of Spirit, where it loses its power and the victory is won. We conquer by surrendering; we gain our perfection by giving up our defects. The Angel of Death and Rebirth is the Causal Power that will help us accomplish this heroic task.

We will return to this angel in a moment, but first I want us to be very clear about the matter of *death*, a word that provokes fear and trembling in many people. In Truth that which we call death is but an entrance into a more glorious life of joy, fulfillment, peace, and freedom, whether the experience is physical or mystical. In each case it is an unceasing flow of sentient life, but with a difference. Except for the immediate uplift of consciousness derived from the experience of being freed from the corporeal body, physical death is nothing more than a change in form. We maintain the awareness, understanding, and knowledge gained during our visit on earth and carry our tendencies and interests with us as we move from one plane to another.

On the nonphysical plane we continue our evolution as we progress gradually through expansions in consciousness leading to our ultimate objective of remembering and awakening to our essential Reality, the divine identity.

The main thrust of the ancient Mystery schools was to help the initiate "die" to the personality and awaken to the divine Reality within. The core of the teaching was the idea that the only true death is physical birth, and the only true birth is the realization and freeing of the spiritual Self. It was also taught that any person who forsakes the spiritual life and chooses instead to live a purely material life of false ambition is already dead—with rebirth possible only through a dying (detachment) to the sense world.

Understand that the initiates in those ancient times were not attempting to become "holy" so that they could spend the rest of their lives as robed monks walking in circles mumbling some mystical chant. They were seeking freedom from the bondage of the physical world so that they could *remain* in this world and participate in its transformation. Their objective was the mass awakening of humankind, but they also knew that this slip from the dream state must begin within the consciousness of each individual, so they began with themselves, just as you and I must do.

The concept of death and rebirth was best exemplified by Jesus in the Crucifixion and Resurrection Initiation. He taught us that we must die to the lower nature in order to live as the Master Self that we are in Truth. In describing the Crucifixion (the Tenth Door to Mastery) in my book *Practical Spirituality*, I said that the lower nature must die in order for the higher nature to manifest fully. "It is the giving up of the personality, a replacing of the human consciousness with the divine consciousness. It is the crossing out of both the objective and subjective planes of consciousness."[5]

A phenomenal experience takes place at this point in our evolution. Since the renunciation, we have been operating out of a higher vibration, a greater awareness *of* the Holy Self within. But at the crucifixion this comprehension begins to dim as the personal consciousness takes on the identity of its source. There is a fading out of one consciousness and a fading in of another, and for a brief interval the feeling of the Presence leaves us and we may well cry out, "My God, why have you forsaken me?" But as the full understanding of our divinity takes place, the "I and the Father are one" becomes a realization. We have died to the old self and can now be reborn and enter the Resurrection Experience.

Let's get very practical about this idea of death and rebirth. When we stop identifying ourselves as part of the physical world of form, break the emotional bondage to outer effects, and dispel the mental illusion of seeing something "out there" that does not exist, we are removing the layers of personality patterns that have surrounded our imprisoned splendor. And when our divine nature, our *Real Being*, breaks through, our lives are changed so dramatically that earth appears to be heaven. The problems, challenges, trials, and tribulations experienced by the lower nature are no longer there because we are no longer living out of the lower nature. All desires, wants, and needs have been taken over by the spiritual Self and are brought into manifestation according to the higher vision, which always means more than we have conceived of in our limited consciousness. We "die" to lack, limitation, unfulfillment, futility, conflict, despair, fear, and guilt, and we are reborn into the resurrected life of dominion and mastery.

How do we bring about this mystical death and rebirth? The simplest way to answer this question is that if we will do our part, Spirit will do the rest—and our part can basically be summed up in four steps:

1. We place our faith in the invisible spiritual world rather than in the visible material world, which means that we must cease giving power to the material plane of effects and reclaim the authority that is ours by divine right.

2. Sever the emotional attractions that are causing bondage in our life. We give up everything to the Spirit of God within, including those desires that are pulling us down, for in truth only when we surrender the desire to the higher power do we acquire the right to have the desire fulfilled.

3. With humility we release the sum total of ego energies to the Holy Self within, symbolically lifting the lower nature into the Light of Spirit.

4. We develop our power of intuition through meditation to where it is greater than the misperceptions seen through the false eyes of the personality.

If we are totally sincere and willing to surrender the lesser in exchange for the greater, the Holy Self will gently ease the old personality out and will replace that lower energy with Itself. I do not want to give the impression that this is an overnight process, for there must be much preparation for the fusion to occur. Not only must the old wine and all that it represents be emptied out, but an entirely new wineskin must be made ready for the new inpouring. Paul said, "I die daily" (1 Corinthians 15:31)—and this is what we must do to secure the final victory. Remember, "unless one is born anew, he cannot see the kingdom of God" (John 3:3). And "whoever loses his life for [the sake of the Christ within] will find it" (Matthew 16:25).

By dying daily, and moment by moment if necessary, we break the ego's hold and begin the ascension to the superconsciousness. We die to the pulls of the lower nature to some extent every time we move into the secret place in consciousness and sense and feel the Presence of God where we are. We loosen the grip of the lower nature whenever we make the connection with the Master Self and see the inner Light, feel the Love, and know that we are beholding Reality. We are in the rebirthing process each time we turn away from appearances and refuse to ponder the challenges of health, supply, career, or relationships.

In the tarot this angel is represented by the Death card. According to *Highlights of the Tarot*, this key means "change, motion, transformation. It is the power . . . that transforms our consciousness and releases it from the trammels and limitations that now hamper its free expression."[6]

In esoteric astrology the angel draws on the energy of Scorpio to transmute the personality and bring an end to selfish desires, ambition, and pride. It assures *spiritual* desire in people as the binding emotional attachments of life are dissipated. "Having reached the new altitude, they can divest themselves of the old, hindering personality conditions, for Scorpio signifies the raising of any faculty to a higher octave. It speaks of death and dissolution, then regeneration and new birth."[7] Scorpio is also symbolic of the Prodigal Son, who ultimately returns to the Father's house and the great celebration.

As you move through the transmutation and the redirection of your human energies, call on this angel to help you in the process. To the average person the Angel of Death is most feared, but to the aspirants, disciples, and initiates he is "the one who is welcomed as the sunrise." Make contact now and ask him to assist you in preparing for the final step of release and acceptance. Ask that your reservoir of unsubdued personality characteristics and binding ego attachments be revealed to you, and consent to having them be brought under control. Drawing on this angel's energy and Power, go back and review the four steps on page 188 and become firm in your commitment to let go of your present life for the greater experience of True Living.

In an earlier encounter with this angel I found that I was hesitant in crucifying the hydra part of my personality because together we had created much of what I enjoyed in this world. I believed that the throttling of the ego would mean the expiration of many of those forms and activities. After showing me the source of my resistance to the death experience, the angel said, "You must change your concept of what it means to live in this world. To live here in joy, peace, and freedom does not mean giving up the things of this world; it means withdrawing your reliance and dependence on those things and placing your attention on the I AM within, the only Cause and Power, and letting the things appear naturally. Those things that are not in accord with the higher order will die and be replaced with those that are, without any sacrifice or suffering on your part. Also consider that the ego does not partake of the Energy of Love, yet the Kingdom can only be manifest through such energy. Is it not worthwhile to eliminate all barriers to heaven on earth? Remember that there is no such thing as death, only a change of energy."

Welcome this "sunrise" now and conclude your session with the following meditation.

Meditation

As I look within and contemplate the magnificent Presence I AM, I understand that the only death that I shall ever experience is the giving up of the old to receive the new. I am ready to do that now. I am willing to take the final step.

I am no longer afraid to give up my humanhood and accept my Christhood because I know that as I move through the fog toward the Bridge of Light,

You are my shield and protector. If I walk through fire, I will not be burned. If there are waters, they shall not overflow me. If enemies should encamp against me, they shall not find me, for I will be hidden in You.

I now walk the path to the Bridge. There is darkness, but I am not afraid. My miscreations seem to be beckoning to me, but my eye is single. And now I see the Light piercing the night and the faint outline of the Bridge is visible. I walk steady toward the Light.

As I step upon the Bridge, I see You, my divine Reality, and with each step we move closer to each other. We stop at the middle point, and I see You in all your glory, a pure Light Body of God embodying the fullness of universal being.

I now take the final step. Slowly we begin to merge . . . and I feel the Light and the Love and the Life. The divine infusion is taking place. I am being Christed. I am filled with the Presence.

It has happened. The sense of separation is no more. The duality of I and You is now only I, the One. I AM that ONE.

I rest now in the One I AM.

FIFTEEN

The Angel of Patience and Acceptance

The fiery golden train holds fast to the tracks as it flies around every bend and glides over every mountain with ease. Fueled by cosmic power, its pace is constantly full-throttled. It is a train that cannot be stopped, derailed, or sidetracked. We boarded it at the moment of our descent into material consciousness and we shall not leave the train until the final destination is reached.

What is this train? It is the plan, purpose, vision, and Will of God. It is the divine process of individual reawakening and the realization of divinity of every soul on every plane of existence everywhere. Its destination: the Fifth Kingdom of God, the realm of Pure Being where Love and Peace are absolute, its time of arrival: at the flash signifying the Christing, or spiritualization, of the collective consciousness and the healing and harmonizing of Planet Earth. All people everywhere, in every dimension and on both sides of the veil, are on the train. In fact all life in every unmanifest and manifest form in the four lower kingdoms can be found on it. It is the Train of Life.

All individuals called human have a window seat, and through the windows we watch the world of form move like fleeting pictures on a wall. The movement of the train past the objects on the screen is what we call time—and the forms we see are only temporary, not permanent, and thus are considered illusory. Let's walk through a few of the cars on the train.

As we move forward toward the Universal Engine leading the caravan, we notice that the people are relaxed, serene, with an easy smile on their lips and a twinkle of joy in their eyes. As we listen to their conversations, we do not pick up any sense of impatience, anxiety, or anger. Rather, we hear words of confidence, trust, and acceptance of the wonders of life. Intuitively they know that the Will of God is life and Love—life to be lived wholly, abundantly, joyfully, creatively, and triumphantly, with Love and right relations as the keynotes. There is no fear of the future, for to them God is trustworthy—and through their devotion and allegiance to the sacred *I* within they have also learned to trust their consciousness, recognizing it to be the channel for the activity of God in their lives. Does everything in their individual worlds reflect this harmony in mind and emotions? Let's look out the window and see.

No, things are not yet perfect, for appearances are not always on the same time scale as consciousness. There is still evidence of nature being violated by humans, and we see crime, drug addiction, and child abuse running rampant. The unsettling stories in the newspapers that we see through the windows seem little different from those in the world of the lower-minded.

We had forgotten that even in the world of those approaching mastery in life, the planetary vibration continues to be more in tune with the race mind, the collective consciousness of humanity, than it is with the Christ Consciousness, which Psalms 46 and 91 dramatically portray:

> *We will not fear though the earth be removed and though the mountains be carried into the midst of the sea; though the waters thereof roar and be troubled, though the mountains shake with swelling thereof . . . he shall deliver thee from the snare of the fowler and from the noisome pestilence; thou shalt not be afraid for the terror by night, nor for the arrow that flieth by day; nor for the pestilence that walketh in the darkness, nor for the destruction that wasteth at noonday. A thousand shall fall at thy side, and ten thousand at thy right hand; but it shall not come nigh thee.*

These are all tough scenarios, but the people on this part of the train believe in the promises of God and are living with calm equanimity with no concern with what is happening "out there." They know they are divinely protected and that the invisible world behind the appearances is gathering force and Power and will soon come crashing through the veil of matter to reveal the Truth of Being. In the meantime they ride the divine rails in peace and serenity. Even when the train dives headlong down a mountain slope or veers sharply at an angle (symbolizing the cycles of life), they quickly adjust to the new conditions and continue in their assured, confident, and trusting ways.

Now let's move farther back on the train and pause for a moment in one of the coaches where many of the spiritual aspirants are riding. We see some happy people, but there are also gloomy faces, teary eyes, and the sagging shoulders of despair and futility. Let's listen in on some of their thoughts:

"I really don't know what to do. I pray, affirm, and meditate, but my body aches, the stack of unpaid bills is growing higher, and my whole life seems to be going down the drain."

And somehow we hear the voice of an angel speaking right within that individual's energy field, but he is so preoccupied with his problems that the words are lost in the whirling circumference of his mind. The voice says:

"You are perceiving a lie. You sense separation from wholeness, abun-

dance, and fulfillment, yet this is impossible. You were given everything in the beginning when you were given your Self, and within the I that you are is everything that you could ever need or desire. You have the Kingdom because you are the Kingdom. By depriving yourself of this Truth you are experiencing an emptiness, a deception that produces fear, that miscreates even greater vulnerabilities in your life. I am the energy that enables you to trust the divine process and live with total acceptance of that which is good, true, and beautiful. Become aware of me, and through the channel of your awareness I will demonstrate to you that the Will, plan, and purpose of God is the only activity taking place in your life."

The passengers did not hear the words, but they were not lost. And we listen to the thoughts of another person across the aisle.

"Despite all the appearances of positive change, I personally believe that the world is going to hell in a hand basket, and I am horrified to think that my children will have to grow up on a raped and pillaged planet. Even though I want to be committed to the spiritual path, I wonder if the world will ever really change. Sometimes it all seems so hopeless."

And again the angel speaks:

"God's plan for this planet and all life hereon is very good, and has always existed as God's ideal working through the evolution of individual consciousness. It is focused will and power and the divine vision of expansion, and it is being felt now by people of every race. Its energy and force will lead to a complete readjustment of values among the people and a

revelation of the purpose behind every difficult experience of life. The work-
ing out of the plan through your mind and heart—through the thoughts
and feelings of all souls—will permit each individual to escape from human
consciousness, and the plan will then materialize in form on earth, and
peace and plenty will be the measure of the world. This is the significance
of the Lord's Prayer. The way of the plan is the divine process, which must
be trusted to the utmost. Live with patience—*not an attitude of long-*
suffering but one of perseverance and tenacity, for the good will surely be
revealed in this world; it cannot be held back. Live with acceptance—*not*
of things as they appear to be, but in the context of consenting to order,
beauty, and freedom, for they will certainly be manifest."

As we return to our seats on the train, let's see if we have learned anything. The bottom line is that when we truly commit our lives to Spirit, then Spirit is in charge of our lives and there is nothing to worry about regardless of how difficult the situation appears. And how can we tell if we have given everything up to the Lord and Master Self within? By the measure of our patience, knowing that every activity is divinely timed, and by the degree of our acceptance, which means to accept our good even when it is not yet visible. We should also ask ourselves if we have consented to having our needs met by the activity of the divine self rather than the ego of personality.

I want to share something with you that has meant a great deal in my life, and it is this: I cannot accidentally fall or be pushed from the train, regardless of my thought, word, or deed. In fact, there is nothing that I have ever done, or ever will do, that would warrant my expulsion from this secret place of the Most High, those everlasting arms represented by the Train of Life. And that holds true for every soul in the universe. We tend to come down pretty hard on ourselves when things seem to be out of kilter, and we look for the spiritual sin, the metaphysical cause, and the emotional block. We think of past-life transgressions, karma, and the guilt that must be punished by universal retribution.

So much of this is nonsense. We keep condemning ourselves because we do not feel spiritual or because we think that we have violated some metaphysical law. You have down days, and so do I. You have felt a financial pinch, and I have too. You have suffered spiritual constipation, and so have I. And you may have felt so out of it spiritually that you were tempted to desert the path and find an easier road to travel. I have too. There have been times when the door to my meditation space could not be unlocked, when affirmations were a bore, and when all I wanted to do was play Earthman with all the gusto of a roguish hedonist—which I considered a form of rebellion against this spiritual "stuff."

And do you know what my Master Self said about all of this? Paraphrased in my words: "It's really no big deal. It is just some old energy moving to the surface to be transmuted. Quit worrying so much about where and how you strayed and get on with the business of living. Just be yourself, whatever that particular self is being on any given day. No one is keeping score on how many times you have felt a touch of anger, anxiety, or uncertainty, and you are not booed by the universe if you are not on top of the world every moment. So stop straining so hard to *be* spiritual. You already *are*. Everyone is, so relax and enjoy the ride."

What I came to realize was that God created me, loves me, accepts me for who and what I am, has infinite patience with me, and that it is impossible for me to interrupt the divine process. I cannot leave the train, and neither can you. The truth is that we are all going home together. So the next time futility hits you, or things seem to be falling apart, be patient with yourself and accept the fact that there is no use worrying about your problems, because everything is going to be all right. Just relax in those everlasting arms . . . and "enjoy the ride."

You have a holy helper to help you trust the divine process, to have faith in your future and the future of the world, and to accept the Will and plan of God as supremely good. It is the angel who specializes in such things, the Angel of Patience and Acceptance.

This angel is feminine in nature. In Greek mythology she was known as Iris, "the golden-winged goddess of the rainbow, and a messenger of the gods. . . . She carried the commands of the gods to men, traveling the path of the rainbow."[1] She was also known as the Queen of Heaven, and it was said that she was the regular courier for the Queen of the Gods, the keeper of the Mysteries—the archetype that we have already identified as Isis, the Angel of Creative Wisdom. Before we go any further, let's look at the code words here.

Rainbow represents the channel or passage between the realm of the spiritual triad or divine consciousness, and the personality, and it is this path that Iris follows in delivering the communications from on high. The rainbow also symbolizes the sign of the covenant as given in Genesis 9:13–15; therefore the Angel of Patience and Acceptance is also the Angel of the Covenant, meaning that an individual's world will not be inundated by a deluge of negativity if the qualities of this Causal Power are embodied. And what are those qualities? It is having a sense of proportion in life, with the ability to remain steady on the spiritual path as life swings back and forth between the positive and negative poles. It is the quality of practicing moderation in all things and dispensing with fanaticism regardless of the passion or devotion felt toward a particular activity. It is the force that enables one to have a focused spiritual direction and to follow life's plan as it unfolds and reveals greater and grander goals to strive for. Could a flood of pessimism and worst-possible scenarios engulf such a person? Not with this angel's overshadowing.

The "Queen of Heaven" reference is to the feminine ruler in the right-minded personality consciousness, the feeling of spiritual truth in an individual whose awareness and understanding is based primarily on higher values. As a "messenger of the gods" her emphasis is always on the receiving and giving of spiritual truths from the Queen of the Gods—the World Mother, or third aspect of the trinity, the Holy Spirit.

This angel represents the vortex, or whirlpool, for the expression of the energies of patience and acceptance to be extended into the mind and heart of the individual. In the early temples of learning "patience" was considered to be more than sufferance and being able to put up with a condition or situation. It was thought of as the Power of persistence, perseverance, determination, and resolution, which could be utilized most effectively after the initiate had developed a sense of proportion between idea and action, a balancing of the inner and outer worlds.

The word *acceptance* meant consenting and agreeing with God that individual beings are divine, the approving of Self as God in expression. This angel once told Jan, "The ultimate surrender is acceptance, acceptance of the Presence of God within as your Self. It is through this acceptance that personality gives way to individuality." Yes, Iris not only reminds us of who and what we are but also gives us the tenacity to stay on the spiritual path until the Realization Experience, or complete understanding of our true identity, dawns in consciousness. When her energy is blocked, usually because of a fear of the future and a lack of trust in the divine process, the individual finds it difficult to adjust to new situations, has a tendency to argue with almost everyone, and becomes wasteful and extravagant out of a sense of futility.

In the ancient tarot this angel is symbolized by the major trump called Temperance, emphasizing the qualities of patience, adaptability, balance, and moderation. According to *Highlights of Tarot*, "Temperance refers to the act of tempering, or the making of a properly balanced mixture. It has a distinct reference to equilibration, for the Initiate must be perfectly balanced with references to all of his vehicles. He no longer goes to extremes, but has mastery of the pairs of opposites because he invariably chooses the middle path between two extreme courses of action."[2]

Astrologically this angel channels the energy of Sagittarius, and in *Esoteric Astrology* we read of the importance of that energy:

> In Sagittarius, the intellect which has been developed, used and finally illumined, becomes sensitive to a still higher type of mental experience and to this we give the name of intuitive perception. There come flashes of light upon problems; a distant yet possible vision of attainment is seen . . . [the person] walks no longer in the dark, for he sees what he has to do and he therefore makes rapid progress and travels "fast upon the Way." . . . In studying Sagittarius, it becomes obvious that one of the major underlying themes is that of *Direction*. The Archer is guiding his horse towards some one specific objective; he is sending or directing his arrow towards a desired point; he is aiming at some specific goal. . . . When this faculty of sensitive direction is rightly developed it becomes . . . in the last analysis, the ordered direction of God's thought.[3]

Call forth the Angel of Patience and Acceptance now and make friends with this Queen of Heaven. She will lift you to the path of pure thinking and will teach you what optimism truly means. I know that she has been instrumental in helping me to formulate goals and to shoot for them with true vision and a new sense of purpose and dedication. You will also love her candid, straightforward manner of communicating. She will not coddle you or go along with your excuses for irrational acts, emotional frenzies, or overindulgence in anything. She tells it like it is, and that is why she can be such a dependable ally on the spiritual journey.

Meditation

There is but one Presence, one Power, one Cause in this universe, in this world, and in my life. It is the Spirit of the living God everywhere present. This Spirit is individualized as me. It is Who I am. It is What I am. I look within and sense and feel this mighty Presence, and I am now consciously aware of the Master Self I am in Truth.

In the stillness of my Being I find perfect balance. I am poised on the middle path between the invisible and visible, master of the poles of opposites, and I see the holy unity of Spirit and matter. I see the invisible domain of the Kingdom, and I see the manifest realm of heaven on earth. I see my path illumined by the inner Light, extending from the secret place within out into the world of form and experience.

I live with patience, determined to follow my path and fulfill my plan and then to carry out other plans in life as my future unfolds. I gratefully accept all that greets me on the path, for I know that the activity of God is the only Power in my life, and I trust the divine process. I move forward, steady in the Light of my Holy Self and in the company of the angel, who will keep me in all my ways.

SIXTEEN

The Angel of Materiality and Temptation

Temptation: "a tempting." *The Tempter*: "the Devil; Satan." (*Webster*) Could an angel possibly be associated with Satan? To correct a misperception, let's take a brief look at some of the controversy regarding this Adversary of God.

A Christian Fundamentalist appearing on a television program held up my book, *The Planetary Commission*, and told the audience that it was "Satan's handbook." We also hear the believers say that Christianity is based on the perpetual conflict between God and Satan, and that most other religions are nothing more than satanic cults. Yet the Reverend Buckner Fanning, pastor of Trinity Baptist Church in San Antonio, is quoted in a newspaper article as saying that there is an unhealthy preoccupation with Satan, that "people give more power to Satan than God."[1] And in the same article Trinity University philosophy professor Peter French says that "people use this belief [in Satan] to give away responsibility for their lives."

A radical newsletter in Colorado reported that the Lord and God worshipped by New Agers is none other than Satan himself.[2] But the *Metaphysical Bible Dictionary*—definitely a New Age reference book—defines Satan as "the state of mind in man that believes in its own sufficiency independent of its creative Source. Personality describes the meaning more fully than any other word in the English language."[3]

Orthodox Christians have also called this tempter Pan—whom one writer in the newsletter mentioned above says is "another name for Lucifer"—yet Pan is traditionally known in mythology as the god of the woods and meadows who protected the flocks and danced with the nymphs. Some extremists have even called him Janus, which is interesting since the first month of the year is named for this Roman god.

Just who is this great tempter called Satan, the Devil, Lucifer, Pan, and Janus? Could there be another entity known by the same name(s)? Has the original been lost in a generic sea of meanings and synonyms, all relating to evil? You will know when you personally meet the Angel of Materiality and Temptation. But before we meet him in a face-to-face encounter, I want to discuss how to be *in* this world but not of it, how to live with your feet on Earth and your head in Heaven, which is one of this angel's basic teachings.

A few years ago Jan and I attended a planning meeting with a group of New Agers for an upcoming seminar, and I will have to admit that we felt totally out of place. Some of the participants were floating somewhere near the ceiling (figuratively speaking), another was perched in a lotus position atop a grand piano, while two more were kneeling in a corner staring into each other's eyes. And this was supposed to be a business conference! There is no judgment implied in saying that these people were not in this world (they would agree), and things didn't get any better when we began discussing arrangements for the program. Both subtly and directly everything related to "materiality" was attacked. I guess I should have asked them what they considered Planet Earth to be.

Condemning materiality is one of the dangers of the spiritual path because some people think they can hurry the awakening process by denying the things of this world. They try to escape from life by pretending that everything "out there" is only an illusion and therefore not real. This frequently leads to a spaced-out consciousness and a degree of negative noncomformity, which renders a person essentially useless as a true server to the needs of the world.

On another occasion we went to a party where only "traditionalists" were in attendance, and again we felt out of place. The men and women seemed to be separated into herds. I joined the male herd for a time and listened to the talk about jockeying for position on the corporate ladder and the latest "I can top that" bravado experience. Both herds were certainly *in* this world with feet on the ground, but for the most part their heads were in the sauce. Life for the herds was a jungle and only the fittest survived to seek even greater physical pleasures in the material world.

Somewhere between the space camp and the jungle village is that great assemblage of Truth seekers and Light bearers who are trying to span both the invisible and the visible worlds, for only then will their mission be fulfilled. Their quest is for spiritual values without material concerns, yet they sometimes find it difficult to reconcile the pairs of opposites—the mountain of light and the valley of shadows. It is to this group that the Angel of Materiality and Temptation offers his greatest service.

Over the years my exoteric (outside world) research and esoteric (inner world) explorations have given me a deeper understanding of what it means to be in this world but not of it. All of us are divine individuals from the Light realm, but we must not overlook the Truth that we have entered into a physical incarnation on earth to experience form, to work off karma more rapidly, to accelerate the reawakening process, and to enjoy life while doing it. Simply put, we are spiritual beings in temporary physical form living in a material world—for the joy of it. Sometimes we forget the last part. I had to be reminded in a dream by someone whom I recognized later to be the angel under discussion. He said:

Live for the fun of it, and die for the fun of it. Nothing else really matters.

Play more, for the fun of it; love and make love more, for the fun of it. Touch and hold and kiss the one who lights up your life, for the fun of it. Why look back with any regrets?

Laugh and giggle and sing and dance, for the fun of it, as a little child without a care, for truly there is no tomorrow, only today.

Be unconventional and nonconforming, a little crazy, for the fun of it. Be a gleeful self and see a hilarious world, for the fun of it. Regardless of what may happen, it will happen, for the fun of it.

Trust the Presence and Power of God, for the fun of it. Surrender to the activity of God in every aspect of life, for the fun of it.

Do everything in life just for the fun of it. Nothing else really matters.

The message does sound as though it came from someone who enjoys playing and dancing with the nymphs (Pan).

Being in this world does mean more than just being ungrounded and oblivious to responsibilities, and it certainly means more than chasing the brass ring. It's also more than coping and hoping, and more than just existing and waiting for death or better times. It means being fully alive and living dynamically with interest, inspiration, and a sense of adventure while in physical form. Emerson said, "I believe in the existence of the material world as the expression of the spiritual . . . the laws of both are one."[4] And Jesus certainly did not deny the world of form and experience. He enjoyed festivals and feasts and the fellowship of men and women. He loved the land, the mountains, and the sea. He appreciated the solitude of the desert and the clamor of the crowds and worked tirelessly in the villages and the cities. Being totally "with the program" of this world, he even paid his taxes.

Let's agree that we are spiritual beings in physical form with our feet on the ground and our head in heaven—our mind is focused on spiritual reality at least to some extent. A part of us is grounded in the third dimension and another part is flying in the fourth, yet we are not totally mired in materiality, and neither are we sailing completely free in spirituality. Our actual state of existence is between two worlds, in what is called the burning ground, where the fire of the divine Self is transmuting the lower nature. Jesus gave us the scenario for this in his experience in the wilderness and his testing by the "devil."

The ancients called this the Time of Temptation, an initiation experience that could last a lifetime if the disciple was resistant to the release of the not-self. If the tests were passed, the individual was then made ready for the infusion of the higher nature and conscious oneness with Spirit. What are the tests and who administers them? In the old schools they were examinations of an individual's personal consciousness, questions to test whether or not the student was ready for the next level of initiation. They were given by a master teacher frequently called Janus. "Janus, *JAY nus*, was the god of doors and gates in Roman mythology. Because a person symbolically passes through a door when he enters something new, Janus became the god of the beginning of things."[5]

As time passed, this "spiritual monitor" became known to the religionists as the Devil, Satan, and Lucifer. *Devil* comes from a Greek word meaning "slanderer"—one who issues a false statement through the spoken word, and we can understand that part of an examination may include an erroneous assertion to be corrected by the student. *Satan* comes from a Hebrew word meaning "adversary"—and teachers may well assume that role to jog the student's memory. And *Lucifer* comes from a Latin word signifying a *light bearer*, which certainly represents the illuminating power of a master tutor.

A fascinating report of the conversation between Adam and the serpent (the Devil) in the Garden of Eden is given in *The Secret Teachings of All Ages*. In the story Adam has denounced the serpent-tempter in a tirade, finally exclaiming, "Renounced is thy rule forever!"

The serpent answers, "Behold, O Adam, the nature of thy Adversary!" The serpent disappears in a blinding sunburst of radiance, and in its place stands an angel resplendent in shining, golden garments with great scarlet wings that spread from one corner of the heavens to the other. Dismayed and awestruck, Adam falls before the divine creature.

"I am the Lord who is against thee and thus accomplishes thy salvation," continues the voice. "Thou hast hated me, but through the ages yet to be thou shalt bless me, for I have led thee out of the sphere of the Demiurgus; I have turned thee against the illusion of worldliness; I have weaned thee of desire; I have awakened in thy soul the immortality of which I myself partake."[6]

To the initiate therefore this angel was not evil, but was a representative of a Causal Power that we recognize today as the Angel of Materiality and Temptation within our energy fields. And the tests administered were statements or questions to measure the individual's spiritual readiness to enter the next door of initiation. Before we meet this holy helper, let's look at the salient points of this basic teaching. As said earlier, we are spiritual beings living in a physical world. We are from the fourth dimension, and the major part of our being has remained on that level, with our mental, emotional, and physical bodies extended into the third dimension. Our objective is to enjoy the physical-plane experience without getting trapped in the fog of materiality. This means that we are to "live, love, laugh, and be happy" without the emotional bondage of fear, guilt, greed, and sorrow. Our role in this world is to have everything without possessing anything— to enjoy an all-sufficiency of money without being preoccupied with "making money," to have right livelihood without toiling to make a living, to have wholeness without focusing on the body, to have right relations without selfish emotional affections.

We are to know all things while recognizing that we know nothing, to do all things with the understanding that we are not doing anything. We are to be materially satisfied yet not spiritually complacent, to love right action without being fanatical about it, and to meet responsibilities without overemphasizing a personal sense of duty. In essence it is living on earth as a witness to the Kingdom, Power, and glory of the God-Self appearing as form and experience and giving no thought to the needs of the lower nature. A difficult assignment? Of course, and that is why we have a particular power vibration in our energy fields to help us along the way.

In the tarot this angel is symbolized as Old Pan (the Devil) and astrologically is represented by Capricorn. In the Mystery-school teachings this angel was considered not only a tester but also a protector of the disciple on the path, for he continuously monitors and measures the growth of consciousness and, as necessary, injects thoughts of caution and discretion into the individual's mind. This is done to keep the person on the middle path, enabling him or her to walk the edge of materiality while maintaining an awareness of the Cause within. Otherwise the aspirant could fall into the mesmeric clutches of deep materialism.

If a particular learning experience is necessary to stimulate greater understanding, this angel may "tempt" consciousness to prove the ineffectiveness and dangers of spiritual pride, of a savior complex, of relying on unrealized truth to correct an outer condition, or of seeking the treasures of the world through ego-prompted manipulations. I know. Before I became aware of the energy and activity of this angel, I was tempted many times, and it was usually in situations where I took action beyond the limits of my spiritual understanding.

For example, following a meditative treatment for abundance I did one morning, a man came to my office offering me a "can't miss" business proposition that promised great wealth in a relatively short time. It was a most tempting offer, and much to my later regret, I accepted. After all, this man had no doubt been sent by God in answer to my prayers—or so I thought. Actually it was an excellent test of my consciousness of God as the only supply—an examination of my understanding of the Truth of abundance, for when Spirit moves through us to appear as any needed thing, there is no possibility of loss or turmoil. I learned that lesson the hard way.

On another occasion Jan and I were offered a substantial gift in the form of land, which we considered the answer to a prayer regarding the building of a spiritual center. The test: Does consciousness understand that the only gifts are those from within and that they are always given without constraints? While the generosity may appear to come from people, the physical beings are simply being used as instruments for Spirit to present the gift *with no strings attached*. We quickly recognized the obligation that would be incurred and lovingly declined. Test passed.

The Angel of Materiality and Temptation works with us to reveal our personal limitations so that we may refocus on the one Presence and Power within. It is the energy that enables us to say with understanding, "I live, yet not I, but Christ liveth in me." It is knowing that I AM is greater than myself, and we let *that* I AM live through us, as us. When this angel's energy is blocked—usually because of a total focus on effects and the fluctuation between an overwhelming desire for things and a magnified fear of not having them—the individual becomes overly obsessive. He lives only in the desire world with a narrow mind and little strength of character.

The Devil card of the tarot symbolizes the nothingness of the lower nature by showing the animal natures of man and woman chained to the

Devil's footstool. It portrays the falsehood and delusion of the ego and the bondage to outward appearances.

This angel partakes of the Capricorn energy to help us maintain the proper structure in consciousness. John Jocelyn writes, "Capricorn has several symbols. The best known is the *Goat*, a thrifty animal that climbs high up the mountain, cautiously moving from crag to crag, seeking the summit."[7] (It is interesting that Pan, another name for this angel, was depicted as half man and half goat in Greek mythology.) According to Torkom Saraydarian,

> The Capricornian energy is a very potent energy, and throughout the ages, great Sons of Light consciously cooperating with it, brought about great revolutionary changes on our planet. The Capricornian energy not only brings concrete blessings of life, prosperity and abundance, but also spiritual blessings, new ideas, contact with higher frequencies, new creative expressions, viewpoints and greater expansions of consciousness. The main purpose of the energy of Capricorn is to lead a man or a woman into transfiguration or into true enlightenment.[8]

Ask your Holy Spirit to take you to meet this Causal Power, or if you are comfortable by now working with the angels on the inner plane, simply call forth this angel and communicate with him as you would a special friend. Remember that he functions as an "alarm system" to keep your head in the spiritual realm while your feet are in the gentle surf of delightful experiences on the physical plane. As you learn from his tests, you will be protected from wading too far out into the drowning waters of materialism and will be lifted toward the Holy Mountain.

Meditation

As I call forth the Angel of Materiality and Temptation, I see his light ahead, and I move toward it with confidence. And now before me stands this Emissary of Cosmic Law. In my own words and in my own way I express my gratitude for his guidance and protection, for helping me to be in this world, though not of it, and to be one with the thought divine.

I now listen to the words of the angel. I hear. I understand.

I embrace the angel in appreciation and then move deeper in consciousness to meet my Master Self. And in this Presence I ponder these thoughts:

I am the instrument through which the Master I AM expresses, and I place my dependence on this Holy One within rather than on anything in the outer world. I understand that the only responsibility that I have in life is to be conscious of my God-Self and that that Self will then meet all of my responsibilities through me. I realize that as long as there is a human sense of being, I must not rely on that sense to free me from lack and limitation. My reliance must be totally on the Christ within, who is eternally radiating the Energy of All Good into my world.

I now live as an open channel for You, my Lord and Master Self, without spiritual pride, without relying on unrealized truth to change my world, without distortions of reality. I will live in oneness with You as I walk the earth, enjoying every moment of my journey and knowing that the Awakening will soon take place. And I will emerge as the one who says, "He who sees me sees the Father."

I now listen to the words of my Holy Self.

(Listen in the silence.)

SEVENTEEN

The Angel of Courage and Perseverance

If we substitute the angel names for their mythological counterparts, we see that the Angel of Courage and Perseverance is the son of the Angel of Cycles and Solutions and the Angel of Creative Wisdom. This blending of the essences of (a) the Energy of Fortune and Miracles and the ability to move into expansive cycles with a totally positive attitude and (b) the Energy of Creative Wisdom and a finely tuned intuitive nature produces (c) the Energy of Steadfastness—the courage to live the Truth of Being and to persevere in that consciousness regardless of outer appearances.

It is Jupiter and Isis begetting Mars. So if you have been working with the angels—particularly the two mentioned above—the Power of courage may already be pulsating in your consciousness.

Mythology also tells us that the Angel of Courage and Perseverance (Mars), and the Angel of Abundance (Venus), became lovers and had a daughter, Harmonia—meaning "harmony." While this is not the Angel of Order and Harmony discussed in chapter nine, it is a derivative of two mighty energy patterns that can bring order out of chaos, at least temporarily. We did not discover this connection until Jan received a message while in a meditation with the angels that Mars and Venus should make love. When she asked why, she was told that the blending of their energies would bring peace and prosperity into a situation. This seemed curious, particularly since Mars has traditionally been known as the god of war, but Jan related the "war" reference to the Principle of Harmony Through Conflict. This principle can at times be viewed as a spiritual necessity in order to free us of ego control and emotional pulls—in this case releasing the imprisoned abundance to come forth in peace. She was told that Mars is the energy that goes out and conquers and can be the active or action energy that impregnates the passive substance of Venus to give birth to a harmonious solution to a problem. We will have an even clearer understanding of this as we discuss the true meaning of courage and perseverance.

"Take courage": This instruction from Acts 23:11, which is universal in its application, is crucial to our journey up the mountain. But taking courage is often easier said than done because we may not know what the word really means. *Courage* comes from Latin, meaning to "have heart." *Heart* is derived from the root word of *creed*, which means to "believe in a principle." So to "take courage" we must be bold, daring, and fearless, with hearts filled with an unshakable belief in a principle. But, and this is a major exception, the principle believed in must be a *spiritual law*, otherwise the very opposite of courage may be manifest in our lives.

What do you honestly believe in? Whatever you contemplate the most, wherever your attention is primarily focused, that is where your beliefs are centered. If you are overly concerned with your safety and protection, your belief is in a law of risks and hazards—in a nonprotective universe—and that is what you will get. If you see more lack than abundance in your life, forgetting the invisible, omnipresent substance and seeing only the tip of the iceberg as the truth, you are believing in a law of insufficiency. Your heart will then express fear and dread, the antonyms of courage, which are outpictured in your life to conform to the limiting pattern in consciousness.

I once had a bi-location experience, a sense that I was in two places at the same time, in which I encountered an old man who continually asked me, "What do you *see*?" He was saying, in effect, "Lift up your vision; walk only the high road; follow only the divine image, for only then will you be bold enough to do that which is yours to do." In the high vision there is only fearlessness and dauntlessness; in looking down, there is only timidity and faintheartedness.

What are you seeing in your world? Where is your attention placed? Where are you looking? We always follow our vision; we always walk toward the image held dominantly in mind; we constantly chase the emotions pulling on the heart; we become what we contemplate. That is the law! If we feel ill, we give the body the lead and begin to follow the signs of infirmity, looking down and seeing only sickness and affliction. If there is conflict in the home or workplace, our minds center on that energy and we are pulled into anger and chaos. If there is loneliness, we step in behind that shadow and follow it into greater depression. If there is unfulfillment, we ride that rail right into the unemployment station.

To "take courage" means to *look up* and follow the highest vision right to the top of the mountain. It is to believe in God and believe the Holy Master Self within—our all-providing, all-protecting, ever-healing, ever-working essential being who says, "Follow me, be not afraid, come unto me, be of good cheer, learn of me, fear not, I am with you always." The high vision is to see the Truth with the inner eye and to hold to it even when "the mountains shake with swelling." We give everything to the Most High within and go forth trusting that Self with our every breath. This is "having your heart" in Spirit, which gives us the courage to walk with confidence into any den of lions.

Use the courage you have right now to look away from appearances and up to Truth. In one way or another we are taught from birth to keep our eyes on the ground so that we can sidestep the potholes, so that we can see all the detours on the crooked road of life. We are told to be careful, to not trust strangers, to be security conscious, to watch our health, to fit in, to not make waves, to not take chances, to be popular. We are programmed with so many *shoulds* and *shouldn'ts* that many of us grow up running around in circles trying to find a way out of the maze.

And then one day a little light dawns in consciousness representing the first stage of our reawakening—and we look to the mind as the way to freedom. We become metaphysicians to find parking places, followed by an array of demonstrations perfectly suited for cocktail-party conversation, followed later by an avoidance of those same people because we did not want to explain how all the claims we made didn't quite pan out. And the courage quotient dropped because we did not have our hearts centered on spiritual principles—the universal laws that would give us the boldness and audacity to walk across the troubled waters without a trace of concern. But somehow we kept on moving toward that distant star, and in looking back we saw that perseverance was the key.

And then we reached another stage of our spiritual unfoldment. As we began to tap into fourth-dimensional consciousness, our third-dimensional worlds seemed to fall apart, as the old false beliefs and error patterns surfaced to be transmuted. The battle was on, but with the commitment to a higher level of life, a Causal Power was activated in consciousness to make us spiritual warriors and give us boldness and determination to keep moving toward victory. Let's meet that Agent of Cosmic Force now operating within our energy fields.

The Angel of Courage and Perseverance provides the Power of true grit and the energy of steadfastness to live the Truth of Being regardless of the combat and conflict going on around us. If the energy of this angel is blocked, the individual is easily angered and can become very hostile and resentful, usually for the slightest reason. The block can be created by an inability to adapt to new conditions and by judging by appearances. For the more sensitive types, a perception of the pain and suffering of the world and the wrong use of empathy can also shut down this energy flow.

In many sacred academies the Initiator who assumed the role of this archetype was called either Ares or Mars, and his role was to bring down his "fire of heaven" upon the students and free them from personality control. The process was based on inciting a rebellion in consciousness through great stimulation of the lower nature—to literally bring forth a confrontation between the personality and what the individual perceived to be the higher self. It is through this battle of values that the student realized that the high road is the only one worth treading and that the lower nature is brought into the fires of final purification.

How many times have you gone through such an initiation? You know the right thing to do, but the left-hand path seems to offer a quick fix, an easy way out, and the excitement of the moment appears to outweigh any negative consequences. And so the battle commences. Thoughts such as "I have a right to live my own life" or "The end justifies the means" provide ammunition for the guns of desire. Then the anticipated feelings of guilt, even on the subconscious level, produce anger that is vented on the closest authority figure—the Spirit of God within speaking as the voice of conscience—and is then projected out onto anyone in physical form who happens to push the wrong button. The Tibetan master Djwhal Khul says that in these situations the disciple must "carry his physical nature, his emotional or desire nature and his mental processes up into heaven. This takes place as a consequence of overcoming the 'serpent of evil' by the means of the 'serpent of wisdom,' which is the esoteric name oft given to the soul."[1] It is the energy of the Angel of Courage and Perseverance that enables us to carry our lower nature into the higher.

There are also times when we know the right thing to do and want to do it, but a lack of courage keeps us in a passive state. Perhaps it is the fear that we will hurt someone and the belief that if we ignore the situation it will go away. But this angel works for the Lord, and if the intention is right and in line with the highest good for all, he will continue to push, prod, and poke until we finally make the commitment to take action. With that commitment comes the courage to follow through. Jan and I had known for some time that the Quartus Foundation staff should be trimmed to be more in line with income generated, but we hesitated because we felt that our role was to take care of these beautiful souls; we couldn't just turn them out into the world to fend for themselves. I guess that we forgot that these were God's people and that the Master Self of each one could never be unemployed or suffer lack and limitation. Jan was more open to guidance in this situation than I was, and when she received the word as to what must be done, she agreed to take immediate action. That's all it took to release the Energy of Courage. She called a staff meeting, outlined the plan, and the people involved not only approved of her decision but wondered why we had waited so long. Harmony permeated the office, and the transition was made in Love and peace.

In the tarot this angel is shown as the Tower and is represented as

> the flash of clear vision which reveals to the searcher the true nature of his being which has previously been hidden from him because of the bondage of his consciousness. The tower is the structure of error and ignorance, which is struck by the lightning of Spiritual Comprehension emanating from the central sun of Truth, or Pure Being. The falling figures are the two modes of personal consciousness, generally called self-consciousness and subconsciousness. The flash of super-consciousness turns all of our conceptions of personal consciousness upside down and utterly destroys these false conceptions.[2]

Astrologically this angel uses the energy of Mars for its power. It may stimulate passion and provide an almost militant attitude to make us prove spiritual reality, and a major battle with the ego usually occurs at this time. Mars energy can also push those most vulnerable into fanatic idealism and fearful conflicts, but the positive intention is always to release the individual from ego control and provide the heart and courage to continue toward the Light. When the needed purification takes place, the "flash of clear vision" is received, the tower of ignorance is struck by the lightning of Truth, and the Awakening process is accelerated as never before.

A close personal friend of mine had an interesting experience working in tandem with this angel and the Angel of Success. Here is Eron's story, based on her journal entries:

"Every once in a while you wake up to find your whole world has changed. Your neighbor's world may be the same as he perceived it the day before, but yours is totally different. Today is such a day because yesterday I presented myself with an opportunity to restore some of the imbalances in my life. For some time the creations of my former state of consciousness had been painfully breaking up, and I had to decide what world I was going to create to replace the one that was falling apart. In the midst of pain, fearful anxieties demand attention from the well-worn patterns of our human mind. I could look at this situation from that old consciousness, or from my own expanded state of awareness. It's one thing to experience the subjective nature of Cosmic Consciousness, meditate on its bliss, or to write about it intellectually, yet it is another matter to bring this consciousness into your awareness. When you begin to do so, you can bet your bottom dollar that your world is going to change.

"It had been several months since I had worked with the angels in a direct approach, and it was time to call out for help. Instead of going through a long process of personally contacting them I found myself instantly aware of their presence as my presence. I could actually feel the expanded consciousness of myself pressing upon the remaining boundaries of my personal self. The pressing came from both within and without. The voices of distinct angels could be heard, but they did not appear in the imagined forms of my objective mind. They stood invisibly, within my awareness of myself.

"I knew the familiar tone of my Angel of Courage and Perseverance, as this Mars energy encouraged me to keep my focus and not judge by appearances—because by all appearances my finances were lacking and my relationships were falling apart. Everything that I had manifested by my elementary spiritual powers was changing form, but I had to laugh at myself, as my own dominant Mars energy couldn't stand to be comfortable for long. My own expanding consciousness had been using the energies of Mars and Saturn (Angel of Success) for months to create this dramatic opportunity for my world to be transformed. These two Causal Powers had worked together to force my conscious mind to make choices. Was I going to live in the Kingdom and continue to reach for my highest good, or was I going to rest a while in the comfort of a life between the two worlds?

"Well, I'm just not good at sitting still. And success at one level does not seem like success at another. These energies had created outward changes that exposed imbalances in my life, so I now joined with these angels to let go of the old forms that were manifestations of a former state of awareness. Although by all appearances this was destroying my world, I knew that this was an opportunity to step up to an even more fulfilling life. Earlier I would have prayed, meditated, and affirmed myself into recreating my outer world. But now I just focused on the I AM Presence within, and the angels pressed upon me, embraced me, as I experienced the new determination and daring. Suddenly I had the message. I had been far too concerned with what I should do, when, where, and with whom. All that I had really been doing was putting stuff around me to justify my blurred version of Reality, and as my vision cleared, I didn't need these things to protect me.

"As I kept my focus in the subjective, there were no longer two worlds, and there was no thought of separate when's, where's, or with whom's. The forms themselves were not separate from Cause. The pain of change dissolved, and fear flew out the window. Forms were now seen in terms of their subjective purpose, and I knew that I was able to consciously objectify my world from my subjective consciousness. My whole world changed overnight. God was now appearing *as* God, and it was now clear that my function was to be a conscious cocreator. I didn't have to resist living in the world; I only had to begin to create my world from the perspective of oneness. And thanks to the angels, what one day seemed to be a world falling apart was now seen as the successful transformation of consciousness."

As the preface to the meditation, make contact with the angel—this Fire of Heaven—and ask what the two of you can do to work together for your highest good. Commune, listen, and write the answers in your journal. Then make contact with heaven itself.

Meditation

Master Self I AM, I recognize and acknowledge you as the only activity at work in my life and affairs. There is no other Power, nothing that can affect me in the outer world, for you are the one force, the only Power. None other exists. I know that you are eternally shining as the Holy Sun and the Light of heaven and earth, and I feel your radiance on me, in me, and through me.

Within the waves of your gleaming rays is the highest vision for my life. Let me see as you see, that I may know as you know.

In the brilliance of your Light is the wholeness and perfection of my body. Let me feel this soundness, this completeness, as you see it in Truth.

In the shining energy of your thoughts is the creative expression for my life where I may serve in Love and fulfullment. Let me understand through your mind that I may seize this opportunity of joyful accomplishment.

In the constant flow of your magnificent substance is the vast abundance that is my divine inheritance. Let me recognize this eternal supply as you bear witness to its reality in my life.

You are forever extending yourself and appearing as everything that I could ever need, want, or desire in this world. Let me realize this through your Power to know, and be free.

Capture the vision, the feeling, the understanding. Recognize and realize the Truth and make it your creed. And from that secret place on high will flow all the courage, boldness, and daring that you will ever need to move through the battles of life unscathed.

EIGHTEEN

The Angel of Service and Synthesis

The mystics of the ages have said that only when the disciple has been initiated into the meaning of *service* will he or she be ready to receive the infusion of the spiritual Self. We also see this portrayed in Freemasonic symbolism: "The soul, constructed from an invisible fiery substance, a flaming golden metal, is cast by the Master Workman, CHiram Abiff, into the mold of clay (the physical body) and is called the Molten Sea. The temple of the human soul is built by three Master Masons personifying Wisdom,

Love, and Service, and when constructed according to the Law of Life the spirit of God dwells in the Holy Place thereof."[1]

We can understand now why service is so important in our lives: It is one of the primary foundation stones in the building of an appropriate place to receive the Master Self. We should also recognize that the word *service* does not mean being a servant, nor does it imply servitude. It is the idea of "What do I have and what can I do to make this a better world? How can I best provide assistance to others without infringing on their independence? What opportunities do I see to promote cooperation, unity, and a sense of brotherhood?" The old schools answered such questions and showed the students how to be of maximum use to the world by teaching the true meaning of harmlessness, inclusiveness, idealism, and universal friendship.

World Service is also the initiation relating to the Eighth Door to Mastery, preceded by:

1. The birth of Truth in consciousness
2. The protection of Truth from the ego
3. Understanding spiritual law
4. The baptism, or purification of the emotional nature
5. The overcoming of temptations
6. Transmutation—the dissolving of illusions to reveal Reality
7. The calling forth of our spiritual powers

At this point we are ready to enter the Eighth Door and be initiated as an adept of service. And what follows? The final doors leading to mastery: the Transfiguration, meaning the integration of the lower and higher natures; the Crucifixion, symbolizing the sacrifice of the integrated lower nature; the Resurrection, representing life being lived in and as the consciousness of the Master Self; and finally the Ascension and the total merging with the Will of God. So we see that only through service will we reach the ultimate goal of dominion.

In the sacred academies the Service Angel was considered a perfect blend of the masculine and feminine energies, and the master who assumed this characterization wore a blue robe symbolizing devotion and idealism. His or her disciplines centered on arousing in the student an outpouring of Love for all humanity, the development of an ideal to benefit the whole, and a course of action to implement the plan. The master teacher knew that a transformation would take place in a consciousness centered on service and self-forgetfulness. All sense of separateness and segregation would dissolve and be replaced by a feeling of oneness with all people—a bonding with the whole planetary family. And as the barriers are removed to seeing the external world as an indivisible whole, a similar reaction takes place within, for when a spiritual principle is applied on one level, it also becomes law on another. As above, so below; as below, so above. Accordingly, as the Initiate realized that boundaries and distinctions cannot exist in a cosmic sense, that all is of one omnipresent essence, a new dawning began on the inner plane, leading to the mystical marriage and the consummation of the

Greatest Work. Through a consciousness of service, the personality and Self meet and become one, and through the marriage there is conscious union with God.

Perhaps the Angel of Service on the physical plane can be traced back to Ganymede, the son of a king according to Greek legend. When Zeus discovered him on Mount Ida, he was so impressed with Ganymede's beauty that he carried him to Mount Olympus to be the cupbearer to the gods.

Consider the "cup" as symbolic of the Holy Grail, which holds the living waters of eternal life, and the Christ cup in Mark 9:41: "whoever gives you a cup of water to drink because you bear the name of Christ, will by no means lose his reward." And the "gods" to whom the cup is given are identified in Psalms 82:6—"I have said, Ye *are* gods; and all of you *are* children of the most High." The "ye" represents all of us, the planetary family of souls who are seeking to realize the divine Identity.

Can we see now that Ganymede was representing the Waterbearer of Aquarius, and the life and Power of the Angel of Service and Synthesis? It is the Aquarian energy that this angel draws upon, and as it is poured out upon us, we awaken to the inspiration of service. We feel the spirit of altruism and hear the call of cosmic friendship with all souls. The word *altruism* is important here. It means selflessness—"the unselfish concern for the welfare of others" (*Webster*). The word was coined in the 1800s by the French philosopher Auguste Comte to stand for the opposite of egoism— the reverse of selfishness, vanity, and arrogance. We enter into that consciousness of altruism as we truly comprehend the message in John 15:12–13:

"This is my commandment, that you love one another as I have loved you. Greater love has no man than this, that a man lay down his life for his friends."

Knowing that service precedes the Divine Fusion, or spiritual awakening, we set out to become more universal in our vision, more inclusive in our thoughts, and more democratic in our actions. Our affirmations are "I press forward towards the goal of fuller service; I am the soul, whose nature is light and love and selflessness. I orient my mind towards the light, and in that light, I see the soul. I am the Plan, and am at-one with all that breathes."[2] And "synthesis" becomes the overall theme of our work.

Synthesis means "the putting together of parts or elements so as to form a whole" (*Webster*). In *The Rays and the Initiations* we read, "Synthesis dictates the trend of all the evolutionary processes today; all is working towards larger unified blocs, towards amalgamations, international relationships, global planning, brotherhood, economic fusion, the free flow of commodities everywhere, interdependence, fellowship of faiths, movements based upon the welfare of humanity as a whole, and ideological concepts which deal with wholes and which militate against division, separation and isolation."[3]

When, in our books and lectures, Jan and I ask people to find their "piece of the puzzle," we are also talking about synthesis—bringing together our individual contributions to form the big picture, the plan. Each one of us has something to offer to the grand design for this world.

With the objective of forming a whole we go forth to serve according to our abilities and capacities, with the Angel of Service and Synthesis at our right hand. As stated earlier, this angel uses the energy of Aquarius

> and its characteristic feature is its love of human beings, a feeling of cosmic kinship with all mankind . . . no one is a stranger or an alien . . . all inequalities of race, color, nationality, creed, or caste disappear. . . . Aquarius is the matrix sign that receives, synthesizes, and balances the forces of all the other zodiacal signs. Always does active Aquarian power give the ability to destroy the old, separative, crystallizing influences in man and planet, releasing forces to produce a new thing, idea, teaching or process. It parts from the past to fashion the future while the present yet lives.[4]

In the tarot this angel is symbolized by the Star, which promises beauty, truth, universal understanding, hope, and faith. It portrays a young girl pouring water from two urns. The great star above her head is Sirius, which exerts the energy of freedom, and the seven smaller stars refer to the seven chakras, the energy-distribution centers in our etheric body.

This angel is associated with hope in the consciousness of the aspirant and with the power of faith in the disciple. Let's focus on faith for a moment because it is difficult to be effective world servers without it. Jesus said, "According to your faith, be it unto you." And "if you have faith as a grain of mustard seed . . . nothing shall be impossible to you." These statements seem to have conditions imposed: *If* you have faith, you will receive the answers to your prayers. So Paul came along and explained what Jesus meant. He said that "faith is the substance of things hoped for, the evidence of things not seen." Jesus gave us the principle and Paul provided the understanding, that is, *faith is substance.* And substance is Creative Energy, the force of creation. Therefore faith is the universal energy out of which all things are birthed, nourished, and supported. This creative power within each one of us is the evidence (the proof) of answered prayer, even before we see the finished results.

Faith is the working power, the shining, of the I AM SELF (the true self). It is the thought energy of the Holy One within knowing itself and its power to be and do. It asks, "Is anything too hard for me? Is any activity of world service too difficult a problem for me to handle?" And it answers, "I can do all things." Who is speaking those words? Your Self! And your contact with your Self puts you in oneness with the faith that can move mountains.

Remember that energy is all there is; there is nothing else. Everything seen and unseen, visible and invisible, matter and substance, is all pure energy and is the nature of all form. Move in consciousness into this real world of pure energy and see with the inner eye the vast energy field enveloping you and pressing upon your consciousness to manifest through you. You live and move and have your being in an ocean of God Energy, or spiritual energy, and you should consciously channel that energy—which is your faith—in your meditations. This will open the way to see the plan, firm up your ideals, and move you forward to serve with Love and inspiration.

This angel's role is to awaken us to behold *faith in action*, to empower us with absolute confidence in the world of energies, and to help us live in that world in conscious control of our destiny. If the angel's influence is blocked by fear and anxiety, we will be dreamers without action, planners without power. But that's not the case with those who have heard the call and are carrying the cup of living waters to thirsty humanity. Look at the millions of people who are involved in environmental, political-interest, peace, social-responsibility, and citizen-diplomacy groups. Notice the weight of public opinion that is being mobilized to use world resources to overcome hunger, heal the sick, foster peace, care for the homeless, and promote justice.

Personal retrospection also tells me that while the Angel of Order and Harmony may have given us the idea for World Healing Day, it was the Angel of Service and Synthesis who prepared the soil of consciousness for the seed and who worked with us daily to transmute hope into solid faith in the successful outcome of the venture. This was also the angel who spoke to Jan during the simultaneous global mind-link on December 31, 1986, saying, "This is only the beginning. It must continue each year until the last one comes into the Light." We can see this angel accelerating the work in receptive states of consciousness everywhere to fit together all of the pieces for a new world picture.

Never consider yourself too insignificant for "world" service. Every time you cast your bread upon the waters in the form of right thought and words, you are contributing to the world. This was brought home to me in a conversation with this angel.

I asked, "What can I do to be more oriented toward world service and to be more helpful in my work?"

"What do you see as the *world*? Begin with the small circle within the larger one, your personal world, and concentrate your service there."

"What kind of service are you talking about?" I asked.

"Loving attention to the emotional, mental, and spiritual needs of those within your immediate circle. Are you uplifting or depressing? Are you listening or lecturing? Do you ignite the flame of joy and contribute to another's happiness, or do you let these opportunities pass under the guise of busy-ness? You must bring peace to every table and serve only cups filled with understanding, forgiveness, and Love. The inner circle is the most difficult training ground for service because of the paradox of familiarity and judgment. Yet service to the many cannot be extended until it is first grounded with the few. Begin by seeing only the Truth of the One in those closest to you, and let the vision grow to encompass all citizens of the world."

"It's like bringing peace and joy into our immediate environment, knowing that this part is bound to the whole, and then moving out in ever-expanding circles to heal and harmonize all that we encounter."

He said, "And do not leave one circle until you have shown by example the dignity of the individual and the meaning of true brotherhood. All souls seek a feeling of self-worth and kinship."

"As you look at the world at large, how do you see one person making a difference?"

"Find that which offers you the greatest personal satisfaction and develop the skill-in-action to use that proficiency for the general good, not necessarily from a global perspective. All activity goes into the stream of life at the point of individual contribution, yet the stream is universal, so what one person does affects everyone to some degree. You love to write. Someone else may enjoy bringing order into a business and fine-tuning the operations for a higher degree of productivity. Another may wish to paint works of art, creations that enter the waters to reflect greater beauty in the world. Others may teach, sing, sell, repair, or manufacture; it makes little difference so long as the individual is deriving full pleasure from a principled activity, for it is in the joy of doing that the currents are stirred, the ripples reach beyond time and space, and service is fulfilled."

I asked, "Are there higher forms of service than others, say for example, work that affects a larger number of people?"

"Truly, the greatest form of world service is to live life in conformity with spiritual truth, for then every service you provide will affect the destiny of humankind."

Following the meditation below, go within and make contact with the Angel of Service and Synthesis. Establish a dialogue, an easy give-and-take,

with questions that will be answered to help you become a true server in
this world, and be sure to record the communications in your journal.

Meditation

*I move in and up in consciousness to behold the Presence of my Lord and
Master Self, and I bathe in the Love and Light of the Most High.*

*Beloved One, I know that you are the source of every activity in my world,
and when I am consciously one with you, I am one with that which is mine
to do. You know every detail of my life, for it is your life in expression
through my oneness with you, and it is your Truth and your Way that I
seek to follow. Let my activity of service be revealed now, as seen through
the higher vision.*

*I see now that I liveth not unto myself, and so with love I reach out to
embrace and uplift all without ambition or attachment—to work in cooperation with the grand plan for the transformation of the world. And I begin
where I am, casting only the right bread upon the waters of life.*

*In seeing only the Holy Self I AM in all others, I give up imperfection for
wholeness, dissension for harmony, dissatisfaction for fulfillment—for myself and for all others. I now bring every activity of my life into alignment*

with the vision and will of the glorious Self I AM, and I live with the master intention of serving lovingly, joyously, peacefully, and victoriously.

I am the power of faith, and I let my faith so shine before all, that they may see my right service and give glory to the Spirit of God who lives as every soul. I will now offer my cup to all who come my way.

NINETEEN

The Angel of Imagination and Liberation

As the creative force of imagination is discussed, be aware that I am not talking about playful exercises of make-believe, fanciful illusions, or unreal pretending. In the context of this review, imagination should be thought of as the creation of precise thoughtforms—substantial mental images in mind—and the ability to use those images to channel energy and release into manifestation the Reality of our true nature.

When Napoleon said that imagination rules the world, he was speaking an esoteric truth, because imagination is the power that created the world. As expressions of the Supreme Being we, too, have the power to image a world—to create, or miscreate. Everything in our lives is the visible manifestation of the thoughtforms that we have consciously or unconsciously created. If illness, poverty, and discord rule our world, that is how we are using our Power of imagination—through a wrong manipulation of mental matter. If wholeness, abundance, and harmony are in evidence, our thoughtforms have been created under spiritual law with understanding and have been extended into the phenomenal world to fulfill their mission.

In the ancient schools the initiates were taught to think abstractly, to build thoughtforms not relating to any particular outer instances or material objects, to see color, shapes, and symbols with the inner eye, and the fluid motion of energy, Power, and force. The masters were teaching the art of *intuitive perception*—training the students to see the inner world of the spiritual realm with creative imagination. The idea was to develop an inner pictorial sensitivity interpreted from spiritual understanding rather than relying on recorded visions of something seen previously through the physical eyes. The reason for this instruction was to develop the power of purposeful visualization, the creation of *constructive* thoughtforms, and the projection of those advantageous influences into physical life. Not only would the individual's world change dramatically to reflect the divine standard, but he or she would cease being a destructive force to others. Djwhal Khul explains it this way:

The necessity for clear thinking and the elimination of idle, destructive and negative thoughts, becomes increasingly apparent as the aspirant progresses on his way. As the power of the mind increases, and as the human being differentiates his thoughts increasingly from mass thought, he inevitably builds thought substance into form. It is at first automatic and unconscious. . . . But as man evolves his power, and his capacity to harm or to help increases, and unless he learns to build rightly . . . he will become a destructive agency and a center of harmful force—destroying and harming not only himself . . . but equally hurting and harming those who vibrate to his note.[1]

So the aspirants were taught the art of visualization through abstract thinking and how to build thoughtforms based on spiritual ideas to harness the awesome power of the mind for good. For greater understanding of this process, let's try an exercise using the inner eye. As a warm-up, call to mind the image of a candle burning and view closely the dancing fire of the wick. Now see the flame separating itself from the candle and taking the shape of a huge fiery ball. Send it through an open window and see it streaking across the sky. Now image a giant Niagara-type waterfall pouring from the sky and see the fireball crashing into the water and emitting a cloud of steam. Continuing the preparation, think of a force of strong wind and visualize the energy of the invisible wind as it moves across the land. Now

see the wind take on the appearance of light and see the light move across
night sky. As part of the conditioning process you might also ask your mind
to show you what love and beauty look like in an abstract sense. Once you
have a feel for expressing in mind a quality rather than a form, you are
beginning to think in the abstract. And now for the exercise.

Relax, turn within, and in your mind's eye see a large circle with a small
circle inside of the larger one. Now imagine (see) that the whole universe,
the fullness of the Kingdom of God, is pressing with extreme force against
the outer circle. Visualize the dynamic thrusts of energy bombarding that
outer ring and see the waves of force literally bouncing off, unable to penetrate the circle. It's as though an impassable, unbreakable barrier has been
established to hold back the Allness of Being. The vibration in our consciousness has prevented the fullness of the Kingdom from breaking through.

The Master I AM is beaming all that heaven represents against the outer
rim of the circle, but we have not accepted it in its fullness, and therefore
it cannot break through the ring. Jesus said, "Behold, I stand at the door
and knock," meaning that the Allness of the Christ within is pounding on
the door of our consciousness, but until we fashion an opening for this
locked-out splendor and accept the finished Kingdom, our Holy Self will
continue to batter the rim right into the next world.

So what do we do? We open the door through proper imaging. That is
step one, which is to make the connection with the Master Self within.
When we behold this Sacred I, seeing it with intuitive perception as the
Light of the world we are, and gaze at it, contemplate it, and meditate

upon it, we are building a *conscious* bridge between personality and Self.
We see with the mind's eye the golden ray of recognition and acknowledg-
ment extending from our objective consciousness right into superconsciousness. It is a river of light connecting the personal auric field with the divine
Light of the Master Self, and we see it clearly as a holy bridge that spans
the barrier and connects us securely with Unlimited Being. See the Bridge
of Light and make it real in your mind. It *is* real because your thought
energy has constructed it on the inner plane!

Once the bridge is intact and the channel open, see the intensely beautiful Light of your Holy Self moving across the bridge toward you, pouring
down through the beam of awareness that you sent up. Now look at the
two circles that you drew on the screen of your mind; identify with them
as representing the inlet and outlet portals of your consciousness, and let
them merge with you to where you and the circles are one. And in your
imaging see the golden Christ Light flooding the larger circle of consciousness and feel the Light focused in your heart-feeling nature. Let your
imagination move up and down the connecting beam, being aware of the I
AM-Kingdom consciousness above, and seeing the dynamic energies of the
Kingdom cascading down like trillions of sparks of fire to your heart center
below. Fill, fill, fill . . . let your feeling nature overflow with the Light from
above.

Through your creative imagination you are receiving, accepting, and
embodying the treasure house of your Master Self. You have opened the
door to the divine splendor and you now have the fullness of the Kingdom.

But in order for this completeness to be manifested as form and experience in the outer world, another bridge must be built, this one spanning the rim of the small circle within the larger one. In the first step we were working with the principle of "as above, so below"—a *vertical* flow of the energies. Now we must understand the law of "as within, so without"—a *horizontal* radiation. The divine flow from the absolute to the relative is an L-shaped process, moving down vertically and out horizontally. Contemplate this idea for a moment.

Once the vertical beam is complete in your mind, the Kingdom has come, and now it is time to bring this fourth-dimensional power into the third, the time for the Kingdom to be fully expressed on earth as it has been in the heavenly realm. Since the Kingdom and the I AM are one, pause and silently say, "I AM . . . I AM . . . I AM" and feel the Holy Presence anchored in your heart. *Feel it.* It is your Kingdom Self extended into your mental and feeling nature. And now it is ready to further extend itself into the third-dimensional world of form.

With the inner eye see your heart center opening to reveal the blazing sun of the great I AM and see the incredible radiance taking place. See the golden stream of substance pouring from you and flooding your world. Know that within the stream is the ray of wholeness, the ray of abundance, the ray of harmony, and every other ray that has been missing in your life. See them all streaking forth as lightning to strike every limitation and transform it into total fulfillment. Use your imagination!

With this mind action you are not only creating by revealing the Truth of your Being, you are also liberating by flushing out the old images and patterns etched in consciousness by the lower nature and freeing yourself from the past. As above, so below; as within, so without. Remember the L. Visualize energy flowing down mightily, Light radiating out intensely. See it beaming down from above and out from within, knowing that *energy follows thought.*

Now look at your so-called objective, concrete world. With your creative imagination can you see the old restrictions and limitations passing away? Can you see the spiritual energies at work in a heavenly force field of Mind, Intelligence, and Power blanketing your world? Can you see everything in your life being brought up to the divine standard? Can you imagine wholeness instead of illness, abundance rather than lack, fulfillment over futility? Keep focusing until you can see rightly. This meditative exercise of beholding the All-Good flowing down from the heart of the divine Self and out into the phenomenal world, and then seeing everything being made whole, prosperous, and harmonious, will totally change your life. Remember that the vision that you are projecting is what comes back to you in form and experience, so control your thoughts, construct your images, and see with the higher vision. To help you do this, a beautiful angel is standing by in the background of your consciousness.

The function of the Angel of Imagination and Liberation is to help the individual strengthen the vision of the inner eye, to see with the mind—as opposed to viewing with the physical eyes—both abstractly and concretely, and to liberate the soul from the dominance of the personality. In later schools it was taught that this angel has the power to demonstrate to us that it is what we *see* rather than what we think, that constitutes dominion; that true vision is the only achieving power; and that vision is the link between heaven and earth. If the energy of the angel is blocked through the improper use of the imaging faculty (mortal-mind visioning, which sees downward rather than upward), the individual will be known as one who is insincere and unreliable. He will be a fearful person who practices deception to achieve goals, one who is a forecaster of gloom and doom because of uncontrolled sensitivity in the emotional nature.

In the old academies the Angel of Imagination and Liberation was known variously as the Lighted Path, Spiritual Liberation, and the Eye of the Dream. The latter was a reference to *expectation* rather than to a sleeping vision or reverie. In several schools this angel—and the master who represented this archetype—took the name of Diana (Roman mythology) or Artemis (Greek). Some archetype researchers say that Hecate—the goddess of ghosts—was also the designation used in the initiation rites. I believe that Hecate represents the shadows on the moon, the lower aspects of this archetypical energy. She stands for the negative side, which attracts undesirable psychic forces from the unseen worlds, whereas Diana symbolizes the higher quality, the imaging nature of Creator-God in individual self-expression. I also prefer to use the name Diana for the Angel of Imagination and Liberation because mythology tells us that she was the goddess of the moon. The astrological energy of this angel is Pisces, a water sign, which is ruled by Neptune, the image-making planet. The angel uses this energy in her work of strengthening spiritual vision and effecting liberation. The Piscean energy has traditionally stood for the death of the personality and the reemergence of the soul as the controlling factor in life. Accordingly the angel channels this energy to help the individual have a greater awareness and understanding of the Master Self and to see the higher vision of that Self. Pisces is a water sign emphasizing the quality of purification that is necessary for this vision. It is said that "Pisces is related to the feet; they are the symbol of direction. In the beginning of the Piscean Age, Christ washed the feet of His disciples, giving them an intuitive insight of the path on which they would achieve their spiritual goal."[2] So we see that the Angel of Imagination and Liberation follows the Christ example and uses the Piscean energy to purify consciousness, liberate the higher nature, and open the inner eye to see the true path and plan.

In the tarot this archetype is represented by the Moon card, which symbolizes the life of the imagination and spiritual liberation. One of its attributes is divine insight. *Highlights of Tarot* tells us that "the way of attainment is the way of return. This is symbolized by the Moon, which reflects the rays of the sun back into the sun."[3] This is interesting because in mythology Diana was the twin sister of Apollo, the god of the sun, who is also known as the archetype of Truth. This shows us that when she can function without ego projections, Diana/Moon becomes the imaging faculty of Reality. While she does not represent Truth in the absolute, she is the Holy Mirror, enabling us to see the Lighted Path of Truth in her reflection and to use our power of imagination to extend the divine Reality into the phenomenal world.

When we feel blocked and totally unimaginative in our thinking, all we have to do is call on this angel. In one encounter with her she told me to take an hour and write whatever came into my mind, not to make sense but to let my imagination run wild. She said, "Write top-of-the-mind absurdities in a completely free-flowing manner. This will loosen the grip of ego-thoughts pressing on mind and free you for creative thought from a higher level." I did, and the effect of this cleansing was a relaxed mind with a new inflow of understanding and a heightened ability to think abstractly. The angel knew what she was talking about.

You can turn your life around through the power of creative imagination, and you begin by making contact with the Angel of Imagination and Liberation. Develop a friendship with her and open the lines of communication so that you may hear the guidance that is right for you in liberating your mind, purifying your emotions, and seeing from the highest vision. Then go back and study the abstract imaging involved in the idea of the L, and practice seeing with the inner eye. Once you see (and feel) the energy in action, spend several minutes contemplating the looking up, beaming down, and radiating-out process. Break the circles and open the doors, and begin living in the Kingdom now. It's your true home, where you have it all, and you have it now!

Meditation

In the highest aspect of my being I am the living Kingdom of God, and with my mind's eye I look up and acknowledge this overflowing reservoir of infinite good pouring down upon me. As I contemplate the divine qualities of all that is good, true, and beautiful, I feel the Power of these holy attributes filling my heart and I claim them as my very own. The law of "as above, so below" has been fulfilled.

I have embodied the fullness of my being, and I now give to my world all that was perceived to be missing. I see the radiant energies going before me to fill every cup and make all things new, and I recognize only the manifest Kingdom in my life and affairs. There is wholeness, abundance, and fulfillment; everything is joyful, loving, and peaceful. As within, so without.

I see myself living as I have always dreamed, yet now the dream is a reality, for I have awakened to the vision of Truth.

TWENTY

The Angel of Truth and Enlightenment

The Bible tells us, "You will know the truth, and the truth will make you free" (John 8:32). And Robert Browning has written that "Truth is within ourselves" and calls it "the imprisoned splendor."[1]

What is this freeing truth, this imprisoned splendor? *You* are! The Greeks said, "Know Thyself!" And according to the *Book of Thomas the Contender* in the Gnostic Gospels, "Whoever has not known himself has known nothing, but he who has known himself has at the same time already achieved knowledge about the depths of all things."[2] Since the beginning of recorded time the awakened ones have said that in our true nature we are from above, an immortal Self of God, wholly divine, eternally living in the Kingdom and never separated from our source. "The Crowning Glory of Creation was not a race of human beings but Beings of Light—Spiritual Beings, Divine Individuals fully ordained as Holy Ones of the Most High."[3]

But this Truth of our divine identity must be realized in the permanent atomic structure of our mental, emotional, and etheric bodies to initiate a chain reaction throughout our individual force field. Otherwise we are only seeing through an ego-stained glass with intellectual awareness or emotional stimulation. Since the beginning of this book we have looked at what we believe from many different perspectives and have seen how those beliefs affect our lives. And so I ask again, What is *your* truth? Emerson wrote, "The god of the cannibals will be a cannibal."[4] Following this thinking, the god of the ill must be a sickly god, the god of the poor must be an impoverished god, the god of the failures must be an unsuccessful god. But you say that you believe in a God of wholeness, abundance, and success, even though you may be experiencing a slump in one or more of those areas. That's good, but if you do not believe the same thing about yourself, you are strengthening the sense of separation, because there is no such thing as God *and* you. All of us at one time or another pray to some outside being to give us something when all the time we *are* that something. We look to Father-Mother God out there to help us, not realizing that Father and Mother are the Power and inspiration of our divine original Self. We affirm to make it happen when it already has; we speak the word for more when we have it all now. Nothing is outside; all is within. And whatever is out-pictured in our lives is that which we are holding as true in consciousness about ourselves.

The God of wholeness, abundance, and success is the great I AM, and until we can identify our Self as it, we haven't found the truth that will set us free of sickness, limitation, and failure. The key to a life more abundant in all areas is to be conscious of Consciousness, to be aware and to know that there is an infinite consciousness individualized right within our energy field. In fact it comprises the totality of our energy field! Our awareness of it comes through our personal conscious minds, the consciousness of the personality. So what we have is consciousness being conscious of Consciousness. In the infinite consciousness that constitutes our Reality is the invisible energy and idea of every visible form and manifest experience—but not just as an inventory in a warehouse. All is in the Mind, in an alive, conscious, thinking Mind, a Mind that is infinite in its range, scope, knowledge, wisdom, understanding, and Power. It is the very Mind of God as our individualized spiritual consciousness.

And in that infinite consciousness is the conscious Self-knowing *of*, and a Self-identified awareness *with*, all Reality, both invisible and visible, summed up in the words I AM. Thus our divine consciousness is conscious of its nature (I AM) as infinite abundance, eternal wholeness, perfect life, and total peace, joy, beauty, and fulfillment. It knows itself as the infinite All. This is the Truth of our Being, but it is only true in our experience to the degree of our realization. Our infinite consciousness flows through us to appear as the perfect circle of life in direct proportion to our awareness, understanding, and knowledge of it. By being fully conscious of our super Self we channel only that which is good, true, and beautiful into our lives. By being conscious only of the world of effects we draw that misqualified energy back to us for recirculation through our force fields to appear as feasts and famines in our lives.

Greater knowing of truth can only come through the I AM. The Master Self who goes by the name of I AM is above mental laws. Its principle for expression is the divine overdrive—the loving, propelling force of God's Will, purpose, and Power; the divine thrust, the joyful doingness of Spirit. When we come to the point where nothing matters except that activity of Self, we rise above the human laws and begin to live in and as that divine Self, and our earth reflects our heaven.

It is simple, but it is not easy, and that is why we have a holy helper who works with us to know the Truth—and to be free, as we were created to be.

The Angel of Truth and Enlightenment was known by the Egyptians as the archetype Ra, a being of sun representing the power that resurrects the soul, and to the Greeks he was known as Apollo, the god of the sun and light. Essentially all ancient societies and religions had a solar god. Manly P. Hall writes that Godfrey Higgins, a 19th-century philosopher and author, after thirty years of inquiry into the origin of religious beliefs, is of the opinion that "All the Gods of antiquity resolved themselves into the solar fire, sometimes itself as God, or sometimes an emblem or shekinah of that higher principle, known by the name of the creative Being or God."[5] And in *The Secret Symbols of The Rosicrucians* Franz Hartmann, another 19th-century philosopher and author, says that the sun is alchemically "the Centre of Power or Heart of things. The Sun is a centre of energy and a storehouse of power. Each living being contains within itself a centre of life, which may grow to be a Sun."[6] This was the central theme of the Mystery schools—to realize the Self as divine and embody this Truth as the Shining Sun and Center of Power.

In the ancient tarot the card signifying this angel is called the Sun, the same identification as in esoteric astrology. The tarot symbolism deals with enlightenment through self-knowledge and portrays the "sun of truth shining into the garden of the world."[7] The stone wall shows us that we cannot comprehend the meaning of Truth if we rely only on our human understanding.

When the energy of the angel is blocked through ego projections that say the personality is the higher power, that God is an outside force, and that reliance must be placed on human nature for survival, the individual will follow only the desires of the ego. Such a person is seen as haughty and pretentious with much self-praise. With a focus completely on the lower nature, the healing energies are diverted, which may result in a general deterioration of the physical system. As the grip of the ego is broken, the angel releases the energy of transcendental consciousness to lift the mental and emotional bodies and establishes a healing vibration in the physical body to maintain health and wholeness.

A spiritual consciousness and wholeness are one and the same. When we have one, we have the other. When we realize the Truth of Being, we shift into fourth-dimensional consciousness above duality and are free of "the plagues of humanity." That is why this angel is considered a major influence in all areas of physical-plane contentment, affecting not only the body but also finances, relationships, and career success. He lifts us up above the level of the problem and into the consciousness of the Shining Sun that radiates the fullness of the God-Self.

I had a lengthy discussion with the Angel of Truth and Enlightenment that I want to share with you. The conversation was about his area of expertise, and it was fascinating to hear him reveal the many aspects of himself. We had been talking, and I said something about being true to myself, and he asked:

"Do you know what that means? It means to follow your Truth. And what is your Truth? It is that which has been accumulated in your heart through realization of the nature and activity of the Christ within. This Light in the love center is the energy of all the Truth that you have accepted about your true Identity. It is the energy, the spirit, of the qualities of Self of which you are conscious. Therefore it is the energy, the spirit, of health, prosperity, achievement, right relations, and so on. *I* have been known as this reality recorded in the heart. It has also been called the manifest Christ, the Jesus archetype, and the Child of Isaiah.

"The child is born as the first ray of spiritual understanding enters consciousness, and it grows and matures with every particle of Truth that is accepted through meditation. This Light shining in personal consciousness relieves the personality of self-government. If permitted to do so through the acquiescence of the conscious mind, it will assume the responsibility of healing the body, removing scarcity, mending relations, and revealing reality.

"This Spirit of Truth is the Wonderful One who performs seeming miracles and who offers guidance through the labyrinth of life. You are told that this creative power is the Mighty God. That is true, for the only Power is of God, and from the heart of Universal Being to the heart of individual being is the unity of Spirit, for God cannot be separated from God. Mind and manifestation are one; when you receive Truth, you receive the Author of Truth.

"This Light shall be called the Everlasting Father—the perpetual, never-ending begetter of all that is good. It is the Prince of Peace, the revealer of harmony and tranquillity in life, and you are guaranteed that this outpouring of blessings will only increase without end."

You can begin to free this angel through a total dedication to living and being the Truth, regardless of appearances—which means telling the truth from the divine perspective. We can say that *I* am whole, rich, and wonderfully successful because *I* eternally is, and to use the *I* in any other way than to reflect the Truth of Being is to take the name of the Lord-Self in vain. This means that if we associate this great Secret Word with that which is useless, worthless, and foolish (the definition of *vain*), we will be calling on universal law to bring us down to that level. To say that "I am ill" or

"I can't afford that" is like the cannibal making God a cannibal. If we must talk about the illusion, we may just have to say that "it" doesn't feel well or "it" is temporarily experiencing an insufficiency, because we do not want to attribute our maladies to God.

On the other hand, we don't want to sound deranged. I can just imagine, after totally overindulging myself with my mother's fabulous food and feeling temporarily incapacitated, hearing her ask, "Honey, are you all right?" And I say, "I feel wonderful, but it is terribly full." Staring back at me, she asks, "Who's 'it'?" And I say, "The it that stuffed itself, which is something that *I* never do." Still staring, she says, "You sound like an idiot. Why don't you go lie down for a while?"

The answer to her first question should have been, "I feel wonderful, but the body seems a bit full"—which puts it all in the proper perspective. We do all that we can do to protect our Sacred Identity.

Again, what is Truth? *You* are Truth, so look at your Self and perceive the Truth. Connect your gaze to the Most High and stay on the beam, Live in the Sun and let the Lord of Fire burn away all previous miscreations. Move only in the shining rays and watch the shadows of the past flee. Arise and shine! Get up and out of the human sense of self and radiate as the Sun you are. You cannot find Truth in books or lectures, because *You* aren't there. You are only where *You* are, so stop running around looking for You somewhere else. The search for the Holy Grail is over. You have already been given the Grail: "This cup, which is poured out for you, is the new covenant" (Luke 22:20). It symbolizes the divine identity, an overflowing fountain that is inexhaustible, a horn of plenty providing you with everything that you could possibly need, want, or desire. The Grail, the Cup, represents the Shining Sun forever giving through an eternal covenant—"Lo, *I* am with you always."

Once we begin to live as the divine individual named I AM instead of as the human called me-too, the Truth energy goes to work with all of the inspiration of an unchained deva, flashing communications to other angels in a spirit of splendid cooperation and opening the Gate for greater and greater enlightenment. Soon the ideal will merge into the Real, and every sounding of the name *I* will proclaim God.

Move into the coordinates in your energy field where the Angel of Truth and Enlightenment dwells and become one with this Sun-Shining Power. It could be one of the most important visits of your life.

Meditation

I listen to my Master Self and ponder the following words carefully.

I have promised you unlimited prosperity, and contrary to your belief, I have not imposed any conditions. I give freely to saint and sinner; it is your consciousness that imposes the limitations. But I have told you how to surmount this obstacle.

As it is written, you are told that as long as you seek me, you are made to prosper. The seeking is the key, for you cannot fully focus on the outer world of limitations while searching for me and my Kingdom within. I have also opened unto you my treasure, ensuring that you always have an all-sufficiency in all things. And when I said to simply love me and you would have peace within your walls and prosperity within your palaces, I was giving you the secret of the Law of Attraction. To love me with all of your being is to draw forth my Kingdom into your consciousness, and the truth of my abundance is made evident in your world.

I have promised you wholeness, saying, as it is written, that I am the Lord your healer, that I heal all your diseases, restore health to you, and heal your wounds. This is not to come. It is. In truth, you are healed now; you are whole. To those who revere my name, the sun of righteousness shall rise with healing in its wings. Think on this and see the simple instructions. A single eye on the Holy Self within receives the Light of Truth into consciousness, revealing the absence of disease and the already-present reality of wholeness. I am the fountain of healing life. Will you not drink freely of me?

I have promised you protection. As it is written, when you pass through the waters, I will be with you, and the rivers will not overflow you, and when you walk through fire, you will not be burned. Even if a host of enemies should encamp against you, you will not fear, for I will hide you.

Stay close to me and let my shield shine through your consciousness to form a border.

Is anything too hard for me? No. And who am I? I am You. Not the human you but the Truth of you, the spiritual You, the one called a priest after the order of Melchizedek, or Holy Self. One day soon you will awaken, and my consciousness will be yours and nothing shall be impossible to you. He who comes to you then shall never hunger, and he who believes in you shall never thirst, and he who follows you shall not walk in darkness. For I will be You and You will be Me, eternally the one and only Reality.

I keep my promises.

TWENTY-ONE

The Angel of
the Creative
Word

The Angel of the Creative Word draws on the planetary energy of Pluto for his power, and in the ancient schools the Initiator was often referred to by the same name. This may seem strange since mythology tells us that Pluto, also called Hades by the Greeks, is the Lord of the Lower World, the ruler of the abode of the dead. The key here is to understand that the Mysteries taught that the underworld of Hades was not the home of the dead beneath the earth. Rather, it was the third-dimensional plane of the physical-material world. Dante's *Inferno* was also symbolic of the sufferings endured by those controlled by their lower nature, dead to their unrealized Reality, and living in the hell of material existence.

The myth of Pluto seizing Proserpina and carrying her away to his underground kingdom represents the mortal mind defiling the divine nature and pulling it down into the realm of objective consciousness. The significance of this story is that after the descent into matter (the Fall), we continued to recognize the God-Self within, and for a time there was no final sense of separation. Later, however, we became conscious only of the physical world, and with this complete descent into darkness, our spiritual consciousness (awareness of the indwelling Presence) was seized and imprisoned by the personal ego.

In the Mystery schools Pluto, the Great Initiator, re-created the Fall from the heavenly state to the tomb of sense consciousness—the downward spiral from the Throne of Knowing to the pit of forgetfulness. Through symbols, sounds, forms, solemn experiences, and demanding tests, the candidate ascended through the ceremonials, leading to the grand climax, where the seeker of Truth stood before the blinding presence of the Living Word and realized the Eternal Now.

The energy of this angel is also called the *phoenix*, which is considered "a symbol of the immortality of the human soul, for just as the phoenix was reborn out of its own dead self seven times seven, so again and again the spiritual nature of man rises triumphant."[1] And in the sacred academies "it was customary to refer to initiates as *phoenixes* or men who had been born again, for just as physical birth gives man consciousness in the physical world, so the neophyte, after nine degrees in the womb of the Mysteries, was born into a consciousness of the spiritual world."[2]

The Pluto energy connotes drastic upheavals and transformations, permanent changes, and the acceleration of time. It is also distinguished by its intense vibratory power to both destroy and create form. And since "the basis of all manifested phenomena is the enunciated sound,"[3] this energy is often associated with effects produced by the *creative word*. Accordingly, one of the Powers used by the Plutonian masters to remove the veil of the spiritual world was the spoken word, first demonstrated as a creative force in Genesis: "And God said, 'Let there be light'; and there was light."

The Bible also says, "By your words you will be justified, and by your words you will be condemned" (Matt. 12:37); "Death and life are in the power of the tongue" (Prov. 18:21); And "Thou shalt also decree a thing, and it shalt be established unto thee" (Job 22:28). Charles Fillmore, cofounder of Unity, wrote, "The spoken word carries vibrations through the universal ether, and also moves the intelligence inherent in every form, animate or inanimate."[4] And Ernest Holmes, founder of the Church of Religious Science, has written, "The word gives form to the unformed. The greater the consciousness behind the word, the more power it will have. Just words, without conviction, have no power, and *just conviction, without words*, will never stir up latent energy. There must be a combination of the two to make a complete thing."[5]

The Tibetan master D.K., through Alice A. Bailey, has said, "Every

Word, differentiated or synthesized, affects the deva kingdom, and hence the form-building aspects of manifestation. No sound is ever made without producing a corresponding response in deva substance."[6]

From these resources it should be obvious why the masters of the early academies taught the aspirants to be aware of the consequences of words on the mental, emotional, etheric, and physical planes. They were schooled in the Power of sound and how words spoken with a controlled mind could literally change the force field around any form, *including the belief system of the personality*, and free the imprisoned spiritual consciousness.

While writing this chapter I became more conscious of the direction (upward or downward) of the words being spoken by various people in shops and restaurants, in casual conversations at social gatherings, and as reported in the newspapers. I began to use the old Oriental standard to gauge the value of speech: *Is it true? Is it kind? Is it needful?* The result of this brief survey was that only a few of the remarks passed the three tests. And I will admit that when monitoring my own words I missed the mark several times, even though I was consciously trying to measure the quality of what I was saying. We are all walking around with a loaded gun between our teeth, and our tongues seem to love to pull the trigger.

I believe you will agree that it is time to relearn this sacred science of the spoken word. Remember, we are either healing or harming; there is no in-between, so even in our humor we should practice harmlessness. Let's be builders of the new world through constructive words and creators of harmony with loving words. After all, our purpose is to escape the Inferno and return to a state of grace—right here in the physical world. And fortunately we have our own Plutonian master to help us.

In the tarot the Angel of the Creative Word is symbolized as the Judgment card (sometimes called the Last Judgment). The obvious question is, How does "judgment" relate to the "creative word"? *Judgment* means "the power of comparing, deciding, and decreeing"—a perfect description of the use of the creative word. We see what needs to be done, we make the decision to do it, and we issue the decree to make the change.

This card represents the spiritual nature being liberated from physical consciousness through the use of the spoken word. The angel on the card is blowing a trumpet, which represents the Creative Word freeing the individual from all limitations.

Using the astrological energy of Pluto, the angel focuses the first ray of will and power to bring about dramatic changes in an individual's life. This energy clears out any blockages between the lower chakras and the throat center so that the power can be concentrated and used consciously with purpose of mind.

The throat chakra is an important consideration here. Traditionally it is considered the center for the distribution of creative energy and the organ of the spoken word, as it registers the intention or creative purpose of the divine Self. You may find it helpful to spend time contemplating this Power center to bring it into a higher state of vibration. Another way to awaken the throat chakra and move it into its natural-order process—suitable for the projection of words of power—is to focus your mind on it while listening to music. Beethoven's Symphony no. 5, Allegro con Brio, is ideal for this exercise.

When freed of ego projections, this angel's energy inspires us to leadership with right ambition. It provides creative Power, keen insight and intuition, strength of purpose, and an affinity with nature. The angel will also use the Pluto energy to remove the blocks of false beliefs and error patterns and lift us above the appearances of our miscreations where the spoken word can be used to correct the condition. If the energy is blocked, we will be one of those highly aggressive "winning is everything" people with no concern for others. This particular vibration in consciousness may force us to create problems through poor judgment and then to seek solutions through manipulation of people and unethical shortcuts. A high vulnerability to legal problems is the result.

To work properly with this angel, you are going to have to be honest about what you really want in life. What are your intentions? You are here in physical life to be a builder, to work intelligently with energy and awaken your latent powers to help create a new world. You begin with your small circle and then expand your vision and cooperate in the plan for the planet. You cannot do this effectively as a fearful human being, but you can through the spiritual consciousness that has been growing and deepening since you made the commitment to the spiritual way of life. So your purpose now is to replace the ego-produced effects in the outer scene with the divine impressions of the Master Self by awakening to the power of your spoken word.

Look at everything in your world and measure it by the divine standard. Start with your body—the first "effect"—and move out to encompass your relationships, your work, your prosperity, your whole life. Is there wholeness, right relations, true place fulfillment, financial abundance? If not, go to work right now to reveal only the divine influence and not the fear-induced images of the lower nature. And do not fall into the trap of thinking, "Well, I'm not sure if this is what God wants." It was the Father's great pleasure to give you the Kingdom so that you would never be without anything and so that you would be eternally filled with the infinite All-Good, not only in consciousness but also in the physical world. The only good missing in your life now is the good that you have refused to accept. The will of God for each individual being is life more abundant on every plane of existence, so if you are not living as you were created to live, make the decision now to get back into the Promised Land.

You begin by going within to the Master Self known as the great I AM. Contemplate and commune with this Most High until you feel the ecstatic vibrations filling your consciousness, then ask the Presence to make the Angel of the Creative Word known to you. Ask the angel what you can do to free him from the bondage of your ego. Listen and do what needs to be done, then tell this mighty power center that you want to change your life to be in accordance with divine Reality, that you want the high vision of joy, peace, and plenty as seen from that higher perspective. Affirm that you do not have to put up with "second best" any longer because you *are* the Kingdom of God and you want to start living in and as that Kingdom.

Now ask the angel to clear the passage through your energy centers so that the power of the word may be gathered at your throat chakra. Feel the power as the energy is concentrated and know that you are ready to assume dominion over the world of ego-effects and substandard living. Express your gratitude for this power-building action and return to your contemplation of the Master Self, the divine Person that you are, with the power intact.

While maintaining the feeling of the Presence—knowing that the Self is present and active within you—begin to view your personal world. What adjustments are necessary to bring the forms and conditions into alignment with Spirit? Look closely at your life and establish your intentions, without any guilt from the standpoint of being "selfish." That adjective means greedy, covetous, grasping, and miserly, and that kind of energy is not in your consciousness. And remember that your personality is not going to do the work; it will simply function as a channel for the divine energies. Even the speaking of the Creative Word will be accomplished from the consciousness of the higher mind using the vocal chords of your physical system.

So that your thoughts will be focused when you speak the Word, put everything in writing. Spell out how you want to melt down and remold your world from the perspective of the higher vision, and from what you intuitively feel is the grand design of your Holy Self. Perhaps I can offer some assistance at this point based on one of my sessions with the Angel of the Creative Word.

The angel told me that he will deal with those things "kept secret," and when I asked what that meant, he said, "That which you have repressed, the personality characteristics that you have placed underground, some to fester and grow, others to weaken and wither." And so he took me into the subterranean chambers of consciousness to see the unconquered defects, the qualities that I could not accept, and the residue of fear and guilt that had been accumulated. Through several days of releasing, cleansing, loving, and accepting, I finally felt clear. And at his suggestion I spoke the word with great intention and power:

> *"I forgive the past and close the door.*
> *I forgive all and resentment is dissolved,*
> *I forgive myself and I am at peace.*
> *I accept myself and I am free.*
> *Let the Fire of the Holy Presence maintain the purity of the*
> *   lesser light.*
> *Let the lower nature be sustained in its redemption."*

I was then told to look closely at the highest and most positive aspects of my Aquarian-Leo personality (Aquarian sun, Leo rising) and to "put them in place through *invocation*." I recalled from Ageless Wisdom that invocation is related to *radiation*—the sending out of energy through the spoken word. But invocation has greater power than mere speech because it includes within its action intention, visualization, and projection. After pondering this process for a time, I followed the angel's instruction to gather my personality attributes on paper and speak the word with firm intention, controlled visualization, and powerful projection.

Next it was suggested that I contemplate my spiritual awareness of the Real Self within through the eyes and words of Jesus—to bring a higher vibration of spiritual energy into the personality consciousness and to "put it in place through invocation." The following journal entry was the basis for my decrees and shall be used as our meditation:

Meditation

I shall not live by bread alone but by every word uttered by my Lord Self, and I will worship only this indwelling Christ and no other, for there is only the master within.

I will let my Light so shine that others may see my works, and glorify only the source of the works—the Christ within. This Holy Presence knows all that I could ever need even before I ask, so all that I ask is "Thy kingdom come, thy will be done," and I take no thought for my life. I seek only the kingdom of God and know that everything good and true is now being added. I know that I of myself can do nothing, but with my omnipotent

Self all things are not only possible but exist in full Reality now as my heaven becomes my earth.

I turn within and face my Self. I love You, my Magnificent Master Consciousness! I love You with all my heart, with all my soul, and with all my mind. And I see only You in all whom I meet, and I love all as You.

All that God is, I AM; all that God has is mine, for I and the Father are One. I AM divine purity, the perfection of the universe in individual expression, and wholeness is my name. I AM perfect Love, conceived in Love, extended in Love, and forever aflame with Love, for eternal Love is my name. I AM the peace that goes beyond understanding, perfect peace in silent serenity, forever in quiet repose as he who is known as the peaceful one. I AM omnipotent, the mightiness of God, the force of the cosmos, and my name is power, the only power. I AM perfect judgment, divine understanding, active intelligence, the one who comprehends all, for I AM the wisdom of the ages. I AM the only supply, the rich substance of the infinite, the energy of all-sufficiency, and the I AM THAT I AM is lavish abundance. I AM divine happiness, overflowing gladness, the living ecstasy, for I AM the joy of the world.

(Now see all of the qualities of the Master Self being manifested and appearing in the phenomenal world in the highest

measure of heaven that you can envision and put them all
in place through invocation.)

When all are called into place, the shining Reality will rise like the phoenix.

Let the Angel of the Creative Word show you how to recast your world.
You have the Power. Use it wisely.

TWENTY-TWO

The Angel of Success

Webster defines *success* as "a favorable or satisfactory outcome or result . . . fulfillment, attainment, achievement." Emerson wrote, "If you can write a better book, preach a better sermon, or make a better mousetrap than your neighbor, though you build your house in the woods, the world will make a beaten path to your door." And Ageless Wisdom tells us that success is the *natural order*, that we are here in physical form to attain mastery over the manifest world, to triumph over everything considered the opposite of success: failure, lack, limitation, downfall, conflict, hostility, and infir-

mity. If all of this is true, why are the writings of religionists and philosophers sprinkled with warnings about success? Why do they say that it throws
a veil over evil deeds, that success is full of promises until you get it, and
that it will cause our pride to betray us and make us admired as fools?

The answer is that there are two standards of success—human and divine, profane and sacred. And that is because the Law of Success is in reality
the Law of Cause and Effect, a two-edged sword that can be used to bring
either penalties or rewards. We always reap what we sow. This is why the
Wise Ones have reminded us that the key to all success is to recognize that
the personality is only a channel through which the power and force of
success gains access to the phenomenal world.

Before we go any further, let's redefine *success* in this manner: Success
is the natural order of the universe, wholly ordained by God as a force for
good to replace the effects of this world with divine Reality—to transform
failure to fulfillment, lack to abundance, illness to wholeness, and discord
to harmony as the Power moves through us to accomplish and achieve in
accordance with the Law of Being.

And what is the Law of Being? It is *consciousness*. Everything in our
individual lives and worlds is based on the tone, pitch, shape, and vibration
of consciousness. Radiant success in every area of life is ours now because
God has already satisfied our every possible need by giving us the finished
Kingdom, which includes the Energy of Success. This Kingdom, this energy,
exists right now in consciousness, and our function is to release the success
that is flowing through the divine circuits but has somehow been dammed

up by ignorance and false beliefs. As with all the other treasures of life, we do not try to manipulate effects to attain success; we seek only to eliminate the blocks in consciousness.

How successful are you? Ask yourself, "What does success mean to me at this juncture in time, and how would my individual world appear if everything in my life were totally successful?" Create the personal vision of ideal success as you can conceive it in your mind. Look at your lifestyle, your work, your environment, your relationships, your finances. Get a feel for what success truly looks like, as it relates specifically to *you*.

Now look at how you have been living. Go back a few years and bring yourself up to this very day. Look at the trend of your life and your degree of fulfillment during those years and quickly compare what you are seeing in the objective world with your ideal vision of success in your mind. On a scale of 1 to 10 (10 being the highest), rate your present success quotient in the areas mentioned above, plus any other categories that come to mind. Simply give a rating to the various aspects of your life without dwelling too much on each one. Then total the figures and divide by the number of categories to give you an average. Once you have that figure—which represents in general how successful you feel in life—you will see what needs to be done. For example, if you have an overall success quotient of 7, then only 30 percent of your life needs to be changed. If it is a 5, 50 percent should be melted down and recast.

It is important to be prepared to give up what you do not want in life and to accept what you do want. Remember that you came into this incarnation to be a builder, yet many people do not build successful lives because they are afraid that they will retard their spiritual evolution or that they will do something that God does not want them to do. Some people even feel guilty about being happy, or having plenty of money, or being healthier than others seem to be.

If such thoughts are in your mind, let's go back to basics and recall that God created a kingdom with nothing left out. Included in it is everything you need to live gloriously in consciousness and in physical form on the third-dimensional plane—and the Kingdom has already been given to each one of us. As I have said, we have it all and we have it now. We also know that God does not become directly involved with the effects of this world, that it is our consciousness of whatever we recognize and accept in the Storehouse that is outpictured as physical form and experience. And the higher the acceptance vibration in consciousness, the greater the form and experience because there are no degrees of health, wealth, and success in the Kingdom. There is only infinite totality flowing out, and we limit the Great Unlimited by the measure of our consciousness. How do we achieve the 100 percent level? By working intimately with the Angel of Success.

The angel representing the Energy of Success in each individual's auric field was called Kronos in some early Mystery schools, a being who destroyed the seeming limitations of time in the third-dimensional world to reveal the divine Reality of fulfillment in the Now-moment. In other sacred academies this Causal Power was called Saturn—the bringer of gifts and the deliverer of rewards based on the principle of sowing and reaping. The legend of Santa Claus came directly from the Saturn teachings in the old schools. The Hindu mystics called this angel Shiva, which means "kind"— a being who destroys what the lower nature has created and restores what the higher nature has envisioned so that the individual may have a more fulfilling life. In Roman mythology "Saturn was the youngest son of Uranus (Heaven) and Gaea (Earth). . . . The Greeks called him Kronos. Saturn was a god of the harvest, and ruled the world in its Golden Age."[1]

The masters who assumed the teaching role of this angel in the schools sometimes based their instruction on four lessons leading to initiation:

1. The aspirant's highest ideal
2. The Self-existing success of the aspirant
3. The degree of the aspirant's service to others
4. Failure as an important ingredient in success

The ideal to be brought into mind would represent a grand, altruistic goal to be reached in the individual's lifetime. The student would create in mind an idea commensurate with his most inspired view of achievement and through loving contemplation would nurture it as an optimal goal. The concentration of this life purpose may have been on music, literature, sculpture, architecture, or meeting the challenge of human problems in a new way, but the acquisition of material goods was not included in the goal. Physical comfort and prosperity were considered the "added things" that would be attracted by the proper execution of the grand design.

The master continually emphasized that all achievement and accomplishment seen in the imaging chambers of mind represented the truth of what the student already inherently was. In other words, high ideals conceived in mind were to be recognized as realities already existing as part of the Self's identity, for the Self is the substance of all forms and experiences. We, too, must associate all that we desire on the physical plane as already existing in the invisible world—as *I AM*.

Service was thought of as it is today—"How can I best make a contribution to this world?" Through this desire to give to others as a way of fulfilling our life's purpose, our ideals come into greater clarity and we attract to ourselves the needed resources to implement the plan.

As far as failure is concerned, the Tibetan master Djwhal Khul says that there is no such thing, that "there can only be loss of time." But D.K. echoes the old teachings when he says that "we learn by failure . . . and a lesson learnt by failure acts as a safeguard for the future. Thus it leads to rapid growth."[2] He also says that we should "recognize failure—if it is there—but then, with a face lifted to the light, and a smile upon your lips, turn your back upon such failure and go with steadfastness forward. The only regret that is justifiable, is based on failure to learn the lessons of failure."[3]

In the tarot this power is symbolized by the World, a card signifying the final and successful completion of any matter. It is fulfillment, the sum total of creation. "It shows that the dance of life is carried on by means of the form-building, solidifying power that gives us definiteness. It is that power which enables us to measure and to know with exactness and precision."[4]

This "definiteness" and "exactness" can also be related to *structure*, which Saturn symbolizes. In an encounter with this Angel of Success, Jan was told, "You want no structure, and without structure nothing is accomplished. Running around doing unrelated things is keeping you from achieving the important tasks that you feel are beyond your capabilities. They are not. The word for today is Structure! Organize and follow through with order!"

The astrological energy of Saturn used by this angel breaks up existing conditions by the force of its energy impact so that the higher ideals can be intuitively perceived. If you recall in chapter ten, the Angel of Discernment was considered the Archetype of Karmic Deliverance. And who gives the orders for the payoff? None other than the Saturian energy, which is known as the Lord of Karma, the one who oversees the Law of Cause and Effect, ensures perfect balance, and forces us to prepare for the future. Another session that Jan had with the Angel of Success is appropriate here.

He said, "Think of *rule* in a different way. Equate it with a *Ruler*, one who has authority. I am the Energy of Cause and Effect. Will you rule as Cause, or be the servant of Effect? I am Law. That is why many fear me. They have not assumed the throne of power and authority and are the victims of an abdicated throne and subject to a life of slavery. That is why there is fear of God. God—almighty Law—cannot be changed, but with understanding of the Law, fear becomes success. Power and authority activate abundance to form the substance of faith through the Energy of Love. The Kingdom must be ruled, or it falls into poverty and decay.

"I know how the Law works. I am the Lord of Karma. I dance to the music of consciousness, unfailingly demonstrating the creative power of the symphony that you conduct. I produce the scenario that you direct. Comedy, drama, mystery, horror. You write the script; I produce it.

"Fear of God is fear of your creative expression. It might get you in trouble, so you don't do anything. My energy acts on that, too, so in that state of consciousness you well should fear God. For you are God, ruler of your world of experience—and a fearful ruler lives in a fearful domain. A successful ruler governs with love, wisdom, understanding, power, and authority and reigns over a kingdom of beauty, abundance, and peace.

"Be governed by the Law, or govern with the Law. The word is made flesh. What do you want to see made flesh?"

It is interesting that in the Book of Joshua (1:7–8) we are told that we shall have great success through three actions: (a) being strong; (b) having courage; and (c) meditating on the Law day and night. I interpret this as meaning to have strength of purpose, to be bold and daring, and continually to keep in mind the Law of Cause and Effect—the principle of karma, which states that no force can be expended by thought, word, or action that does not have a corresponding effect.

The Saturnian energy used by the Angel of Success is also called the

Energy of Opportunity, and it brings about the destruction of anything that hinders the individual from expressing the higher ideals. It provides us with the opportunity for choices—to accept our highest good and reject the old, and upon rejection the old passes away, thus is "destroyed" in an occult sense. With its radiating and attracting powers, it helps us to determine our "true place" career through an understanding of structure and the ability to be resourceful, practical, and responsible. The energy gives us discipline, a spirit of cooperation, good reasoning ability, and a strong sense of honor and integrity.

When the energy of this angel is blocked, there is no inspiration. There is low self-worth, a feeling of inferiority, and a sense of being dominated by others—with many failure experiences in the activities of life. But success is *natural* when ego projections have been removed, which means that in the divine scheme of things we cannot have any hopes, wishes, or dreams that have not already been met and fulfilled on the inner planes of consciousness.

Make contact with the angel and ask how you are limiting your own success. Let him show you any false beliefs that may be blocking the flow from his perspective. And with his assistance you might also check your intuitive nature by stating, "I intuitively feel that the following misperceptions in my consciousness are limiting my success in life," and write down what you feel. Look at all of your error patterns, your fears, your feelings of guilt. Be willing to give them all up and then do so by releasing them to the Holy Fire of the Master Self within.

In my first visit with the Angel of Success I saw only a pillar of light with no form or features, and when I asked what I could do to help him manifest success in my life, he said, "Feel me." I thought he meant to feel like success, and when I began to work with this idea in my feeling nature, he said, "No! *Feel* me. Embrace me!"

As I walked closer to touch the light, I saw the faint outline of a form, and I embraced it. It was soft and mushy.

And he said, "You are feeling your definition of success . . . no firmness, little that can be considered substantial. What are your intentions in life?"

I said, "To realize the Truth of Being, to be completely infused with the energy of the divine consciousness."

He said, "That is inevitable for everyone. Now, how do you want to live in the phenomenal world during this process? What do you want to do, for *you*? What do *you* want in and from this physical world? Bring down the soul vision and describe your ideal life to me."

I began to think about those "pressings" from within, and as I did, the angel began to appear in sharper focus: the figure of a large man but with a distinctly feminine face, red from head to toe on one side and blue from head to toe on the other.

He spoke: "I am moldable, impressionable, for I am subjective to you. I become your vibration and I remove everything unlike your vibration in your world. If your energy is hostile, I remove opportunities to experience love; if your energy is loving, I remove the possibilities of hostility. I follow the orders of your consciousness. If there is vacillation, as in your consciousness of success, I will vacillate between seeming triumphs and disappointments."

"What is success?" I asked.

"That which you feel that you have accomplished at any given point in time, and the joy of living while working toward the accomplishment. What do you want to achieve in your life, as an individual, before your transition? And what kind of life would bring you the greatest joy while you are in the process of achieving? As you become firm in your rules for living, for the *way* you live, I will become firm as the law of your vision. I ask you again, what do *you* want to do and how do *you* want to live?"

I let it all pour out, revealing every desire and dream. I painted a canvas, so to speak, of what success meant to me and the kind of life that I wanted to live while I was working toward those accomplishments.

When I finished, he said, "Let every seed be sown to reflect and support only this ideal, for every action that you take in thought, word, and deed I will provide the reaction in the world of form. I will remove that which does not reflect the ideal and will bind on earth that which you have structured in mind as the ideal."

Meditation

There is only One Self throughout the infinite reaches of the universe, the Selfhood of God, and I am an indivisible part of that Whole. The I AM THAT I AM is God knowing itself as God; it is God knowing itself as individual being; it is my individual being knowing itself as I AM. I AM the willpower of God to individualize.

All that the Universal Presence of God has is mine, for God and the expressions of God cannot be separated. They are forever one, and therefore I live in the Eternal Now with the Infinite All, and nothing is missing in my life. I AM the power of God to have.

There is only one Mind, the Mind of God, and no other mind exists. God's mind is the mind of my Holy Self, and my thoughts possess the authority of the Master Mind I AM. I think with the mind of Christ.

There is only one life, ever leaping forward in spirals of new joy, beauty, and experiences. That life is God's life; God's life is my life, pure, perfect, whole. In my divine sensitivity I feel the rhythm of divine life pulsating through me.

I am the fiery strength of God, the living force of vitality that goes forth with divine intention and authority. My creativity is Love in action, and everything that I do is victorious. My divine power is the thought that I WILL, and every door swings open before that power.

I have divine aspiration to fulfill my highest destiny, and with enthusiasm I move forward, forever illuminated by the higher vision. I see that which is mine to do, and I do it with ease, devotion, and gladness, and I am blessed with the treasures of heaven, for that is what I SEE.

I walk in the footsteps of my Self, and my path is sure. My ideals have been formulated in the crucible of my mind and are forged in divine design in my heart. In joyful freedom I now follow my heart, for I have seen my destiny, and what I see, I KNOW.

I am enjoying the fullness of unlimited success, for I am in my true place, doing what I love and loving what I do, for the good of all. I am the spirit of accomplishment, the force of achievement, and every activity of my life now reflects the ideals of victory, beauty, harmony, and abundance, for that is what I BELIEVE.

(Now I ask you to imagine that you are standing behind a door, and on the other side of the door is the divine conference room of your consciousness. In the center of the room is a large round table, and seated at the table are all the angels of the Kingdom—the radiant rays of the Sun-Self, the living energies of the Master Mind within, your Causal Powers. They have taken recognizable form and have assembled in preparation for the first Council of Twenty-Two, with you presiding. As you open the door, you are greeted with a standing ovation, and as you walk around the table, you are given a loving embrace by each one.

There is much joy and gladness, for you have finally come home. And the angels are singing.)

APPENDIX A

Chart of the Angels

1. **Angel of Unconditional Love and Freedom.** *Purpose*: teaches harmlessness and functions as the fountain for the outpouring of Universal Love; serves as the master of the other Causal Powers; assists in the realization of your True Self and the recognition of that Self in others. *Negative traits from ego projection*: fear, guilt, a feeling of repression; a consciousness that says that you are not judged fairly by others. *Energy blocked because of*: judging other people and conditions based on appearances.

2. **Angel of Illusion and Reality.** *Purpose*: helps you to separate false

from true in your life through the energy of creative intelligence; the illuminating principle which releases the mind from bondage and enables one to be aware of the divine plan. *Negative traits from ego projection:* deception, manipulation, dishonesty; an adversary to spiritual consciousness. *Energy blocked because of*: a tendency to worry about everything, leading to unscrupulous behavior to correct the situation.

3. **Angel of Creative Wisdom.** *Purpose*: the ability to solve problems quickly; imparts spiritual wisdom to your consciousness by providing the bridge between the higher and lower natures; ensures that judgment is clear and correct; stimulates instinctive action. *Negative traits from ego projection*: a confused mind, leading to errors in judgment and poor decision making. *Energy blocked because of*: a totally mental attitude that relies on reasoning and rational thinking and discounts the importance of hunches and intuitive feelings.

4. **Angel of Abundance.** *Purpose*: the distributor of divine substance embodying all supply, Love, beauty, and Power in constant radiation. *Negative traits from ego projection*: Financial lack and limitation, family discord, feelings of insecurity and futility; sexual and career problems. *Energy blocked because of*: A belief in the lie of insufficiency, a denial of the Truth of omnipresent abundance, beauty, and well-being.

5. **Angel of Power and Authority.** *Purpose*: great energy and determination, strong decisiveness with reliance on the Will of God in every situation. *Negative traits from ego projection*: arrogant, condescending, self-serving; vain and pretentious. *Energy blocked because of*: spiritual pride;

one who thinks he "has the power" while others do not; an unconscious fear of divine will, thus an inability to totally surrender to Spirit.

6. **Angel of Spiritual Understanding.** *Purpose*: lifts vibration of consciousness to level of spiritual perception. It is the energy of openmindedness, enabling the aspirant to learn deep esoteric truths and become a teacher of knowledge. *Negative traits from ego projection*: opinionated, stubborn, obstinate; an unyielding personality. *Energy blocked because of*: a know-it-all attitude, an inflexibility regarding new ideas and teachings.

7. **Angel of Loving Relationships.** *Purpose*: ensures that you make the correct choice in relationships; the primary energy in courtship and marriage. *Negative traits from ego projection*: poor decisions and wrong choices in relationships; unrequited love; sexual problems. *Energy blocked because of*: a feeling of unworthiness; guilt and the belief in the necessity of punishment for past misdeeds; fear of rejection.

8. **Angel of Victory and Triumph.** *Purpose*: the energy of achievement and the archetype of the conqueror; helps you to meet your objective with determination; stimulates tenacity and resolution. *Negative traits from ego projection*: no compassion or tenderness, an indifferent personality; little concern for others; the energy of the bully. *Energy blocked because of*: fear of failure; a sense of futility in meeting goals; a feeling of low achievement in life.

9. **Angel of Order and Harmony.** *Purpose*: the peace vibration in consciousness; helps you to maintain balance and fairness in all situations; inspires you to live with integrity. *Negative traits from ego projection*: one

who enjoys the idea of conflict, an antagonist, a creator of disorder; a person who experiences much opposition in life. *Energy blocked because of*: an absence of joy and inspiration; a belief that attack is justified for self-protection, that peace and conciliation are signs of weakness.

10. **Angel of Discernment.** *Purpose*: this angel works best in moments of solitude to train your mind to be prudent and judicious and to help you to take actions based on proper discernment. *Negative traits from ego projection*: careless, incautious, and impetuous behavior and speech; a tactless personality; may also show up as an emotionless, uncaring person, overprotective of privacy. *Energy blocked because of*: a consciousness focused almost entirely on the "effects" of this world rather than on the Cause; feelings of insecurity around people; a strong desire for separateness because of uncertainty in dealing with people.

11. **Angel of Cycles and Solutions.** *Purpose*: the ability to accept change and move into expansive cycles with the attitude that nothing but absolute good is taking place; also called the Energy of Miracles. *Negative traits from ego projection*: egotistical, vain, and pompous; one who uses arrogance to mask a fear of the future; a roller-coaster life of happiness and despair. *Energy blocked because of*: an unconscious fear that something "bad" is about to happen; an overemphasis on security and the status quo; a belief in the duality of good and evil.

12. **Angel of Spiritual Strength and Will.** *Purpose*: helps you to have the mental will, emotional determination, and physical fortitude to follow the spiritual path regardless of worldly temptations. *Negative traits based*

on ego projection: a defiant, disrespectful personality; a state of mind that seems to be eternally caught in the struggles of life. *Energy blocked because of*: lack of commitment to the spiritual way of life; a belief that the world of form offers greater pleasure than the inner world of Spirit, thus weakening the resolve to stay firmly on the path.

13. **Angel of Renunciation and Regeneration.** *Purpose*: provides the energy of surrender, showing you the ease and beauty of "having nothing in order to possess everything." *Negative traits from ego projection*: the "victim" consciousness; a suspicious nature and a feeling of being everyone's prey; a jealous person. *Energy blocked because of*: deep-seated fear of loss; an unconscious belief that release to Spirit means deprivation; high anxiety regarding the surrender of humanhood in order to achieve mastery.

14. **Angel of Death and Rebirth.** *Purpose*: called the energy of metamorphosis, this angel helps you to cross out the ego and realize your identity as a spiritual being. *Negative traits from ego projection*: an unnatural preoccupation with the physical body; a health fanatic who is constantly monitoring the physical system to see what is wrong. *Energy blocked because of*: a fear of the death of the ego; a belief that the metamorphosis from personality to individuality will eliminate the physical form; identification with the body as the Self.

15. **Angel of Patience and Acceptance.** *Purpose*: provides the energy that enables you to trust the divine process with total acceptance of "come what may," living day to day with calm equanimity. *Negative traits from ego projection*: difficulty in adjusting to new situations and conditions; also

a tendency toward wastefulness and extravagance; one who likes to argue. *Energy blocked because of*: a fear of the future, unconsciously feeling that the Will of God is not absolutely good; lack of trust in the plan and purpose of Spirit for individual beings.

16. **Angel of Materiality and Temptation.** *Purpose*: helps you to "stay gounded" until you are spiritually ready to awaken into fourth-dimensional consciousness while protecting you from going too far with a preoccupation with effects. *Negative traits from ego projection*: an obsessive person, one who is dominated by desires, yet with little strength of character; considered small- or narrow-minded; in the extreme a violent person. *Energy blocked because of*: a preoccupation with the world of effects; a fluctuation between overwhelming desire for things and overwhelming fear of not having them; uneasy in solitude and indifferent to meditation.

17. **Angel of Courage and Perseverance.** *Purpose*: provides the energy of steadfastness—the courage to live only the Truth of Being and to persevere in that consciousness regardless of what is going on around you. *Negative traits from ego projection*: an angry person, easily irritated; a consciousness of resentment and hostility. *Energy blocked because of*: a perception of the pain and suffering of individuals and the world in general; the wrong use of empathy and the judging of appearances as real causing the aspirant to be "on the side of the sufferer."

18. **Angel of Service and Synthesis.** *Purpose*: to motivate you to greater service to the world and help you to understand why service is a primary requisite for receiving the Energy of the Master Self. *Negative traits from*

ego projection: a dreamer without action, a planner without power; one whose feelings are easily hurt, usually ineffective and helpless in demanding situations. *Energy blocked because of*: a consciousness of fear and anxiety, with faith placed more on misfortune than fortune—"if anything can go wrong, it will."

19. **Angel of Imagination and Liberation.** *Purpose*: teaches you to image abstractly and see with the inner eye; strengthens the spiritual vision enabling you to see the Truth of the finished Kingdom—a higher vision of Reality that can be fully manifest on the third-dimensional plane. *Negative traits from ego projection*: an insincere, unreliable person who practices deception to achieve goals; a forecaster of doom. *Energy blocked because of*: improper use of the faculty of imagination; mortal mind vision, which sees downward rather than upward; an emotional system bound in fear.

20. **Angel of Truth and Enlightenment.** *Purpose*: seeks to unite the lower and higher natures; the energy of the transcendental consciousness, where individuality replaces personality; the healing energy to maintain wholeness of body. *Negative traits from ego projection*: a totally "human" consciousness, ego-dominated with motives based on the desires of the lower nature. Haughty and pretentious with much self-praise; frequently ill with many physical complaints. *Energy blocked because of*: the personality seen as the higher power, with God an outside force; a reliance on the ego as the power within, thus blocking spiritual Light and healing energies radiating into mind and body.

21. **Angel of the Creative Word.** *Purpose*: releases energy to move con-

sciousness above miscreations into the realm of Cause, where the spoken word can be used to correct situations and settle matters for the good of all. *Negative traits from ego projection*: a vulnerability to legal problems; one who creates problems through poor judgment and seeks solutions through third-dimensional manipulation. *Energy blocked because of*: the establishment of material and physical goals as the dominant priorities in life; a "play to win" consciousness based on aggressive action, with no concern for others.

22. **Angel of Success.** *Purpose*: provides the energy to be truly successful in your field of "true place"—the energy of dominion through self-knowledge. *Negative traits from ego projection*: apathy, lethargy, no inspiration, laziness. *Energy blocked because of*: a feeling of inferiority and being dominated by others; low self-worth.

Archetypal, Planetary, and Symbolic References

Angel	Archetype	Planetary Energy	Symbolic (Tarot)
Unconditional Love and Freedom	Tao, Krishna, Master of Heaven, Spirit	Uranus	The Fool
Illusion and Reality	Hermes, Mercury	Mercury	The Magician

Angel	Archetype	Planetary Energy	Symbolic (Tarot)
Creative Wisdom	Isis	Moon	The High Priestess
Abundance	Aphrodite, Venus	Venus	The Empress
Power and Authority	Osiris, Hercules, Jehovah	Aries	The Emperor
Spiritual Understanding	The Grand Master	Taurus	The High Priest
Loving Relationships	Anubis	Gemini	The Lovers
Victory and Triumph	Serapis	Cancer	The Chariot
Order and Harmony	Athena, Minerva	Libra	Justice
Discernment	Adonis	Virgo	The Hermit

Angel	Archetype	Planetary Energy	Symbolic (Tarot)
Cycles and Solutions	Zeus, Jupiter	Jupiter	The Wheel of Fortune
Spiritual Strength and Will	Daughter of the Flaming Sword	Leo	Strength
Renunciation and Regeneration	Poseidon, Neptune	Neptune	The Hanged Man
Death and Rebirth	Thanatos, Death	Scorpio	Death
Patience and Acceptance	Iris, Queen of Heaven	Sagittarius	Temperance
Materiality and Temptation	Janus, the Tempter	Capricorn	Old Pan
Courage and Perseverance	Ares, Mars	Mars	The Tower
Service and Synthesis	Ganymede	Aquarius	The Star

Angel	Archetype	Planetary Energy	Symbolic (Tarot)
Imagination and Liberation	Artemis, Diana	Pisces	The Moon
Truth and Enlightenment	Apollo, Ra	Sun	The Sun
Creative Word	Hades, Pluto, Phoenix	Pluto	The Judgment
Success	Kronos, Saturn	Saturn	The World

Relating the Angels to the Physical Body

If the energy from any particular angel is blocked, you may feel a reaction in the part of the body that corresponds to it. For example, lower-back pain could mean that you are focusing on the illusion of scarcity rather than on the Reality of omnipresent substance, thus screening out the Power and influence of the Angel of Abundance. Whenever you feel weakness or discomfort in any area of the body, it would be wise to talk to the appropriate angel and see what you can do to remove the ego projections.

Physical Body	Angel
Circulatory system, including heart tone, arteries, and capillaries; blood pressure, cholesterol. Central nervous system, which includes the brain and spinal cord; headaches, sleep disorder	The Angel of Unconditional Love and Freedom
Respiratory system, which includes the nose, trachea, and lungs; colds, congestion. Overall nervous system, alertness, concentration	The Angel of Illusion and Reality
Breasts; digestive system including stomach and intestines; cramping, nausea, indigestion	The Angel of Creative Wisdom
Throat, kidneys, lower back (lumbar); inflammation, pain	The Angel of Abundance
Head, face, facial bones; headaches, head-related allergies	The Angel of Power and Authority
Throat, neck, larynx, thyroid gland; nervousness, weight problems	The Angel of Spiritual Understanding
Eyes, ears, lungs, hands, arms, shoulders; sight, hearing, congestion, strains, fractures	The Angel of Loving Relationships

Physical Body	*Angel*
Breast, chest, stomach and digestive organs; abdominal soreness, indigestion, ulcers	The Angel of Victory and Triumph
Kidneys, loins, bones and skin of lumbar region; waste accumulation, high blood pressure, back pain	The Angel of Order and Harmony
Bowel tract, intestines, nervous system; constipation, diarrhea, colitis	The Angel of Discernment
Liver, pituitary gland; infections, jaundice, cirrhosis, physical growth	The Angel of Cycles and Solutions
Heart, spine, back; heart problems, hardening of arteries, heart attacks, back pain	The Angel of Spiritual Strength and Will
General nervous system, thalamus; emotional control, brain activity relating to sensory impulses	The Angel of Renunciation and Regeneration
Urinary and sexual organs, reproductive system; cystitis, vaginitis, impotence, sterility	The Angel of Death and Rebirth

Physical Body	*Angel*
Hips, thighs, liver; excess weight in hips and thighs, soreness, inflammation, liver infections	The Angel of Patience and Acceptance
Knees, bones, joints, teeth; rheumatism, arthritis, dental problems	The Angel of Materiality and Temptation
Adrenal glands, urogenital system, ovaries, testes; difficulty adjusting to stress; fear; sexual problems	The Angel of Courage and Perseverance
Shins, ankles, legs, blood and circulation; fractures, bruises, sprains, varicose veins	The Angel of Service and Synthesis
Feet and toes, lymphatic system; athlete's foot, blisters, calluses, ingrown toenails, poor circulation	The Angel of Imagination and Liberation
Heart, back, endocrine gland; heart problems, back pain, infections	The Angel of Truth and Enlightenment
Circulatory system, reproductive system; weak capillaries, impaired heart, poor sexual response	The Angel of the Creative Word

Physical Body	*Angel*
Skin, hair, the skeletal structure; poor skin tone, excessive wrinkles, unnatural hair loss, easily breakable bones	The Angel of Success

APPENDIX D

Angel Relationships

In our research Jan and I have discovered that prior to asking certain angels to work together to help us realize our highest potentials in their particular areas, it is wise to determine if they can join forces harmoniously. Many of the angels have similar vibrations and are naturally cooperative. However, if one of them has an active energy and the other a passive we have found it wise to ask them to balance their energies as one for maximum effectiveness. This balancing of masculine-feminine qualities forms a marriage or union, with the active energy learning how to receive as well as give, and the passive energy recognizing its power to be assertive and express fully.

Those angels with completely different vibrations may need to harmonize their energies in order to work together side by side as a team. Understand that the conflicting energy patterns simply represent their opposite functions. For example, look at the Angel of Order and Harmony and the Angel of Power and Authority. One is focused on balance and stability with emphasis on maintaining peace, while the other is totally audacious and oriented toward incessant action. Since their "personalities" are further colored by your ego energy, the Angel of Order and Harmony may tell you that you have polluted the Energy of Power and Authority with so much spiritual pride that your decision to find greater peace of mind will be thwarted at every turn. "Athena" may say that she does not want to work with "Osiris" until he has found a measure of humility, which means that you have some work to do on yourself before the Agent of Power is pure enough to collaborate with the other angels.

The angels will tell you what personality characteristics must be brought under control, and once you have taken the necessary steps to clear your consciousness, your role will be to bring the angels together and ask them to make friends and respect each other's qualities. You will learn all of these aspects for yourself, which is what makes the angel work so worthwhile. In the meantime, familiarization with these groupings will save you time and energy.

Angels that are naturally harmonious with each other because of similar vibrations:

Angel of Abundance—Angel of Order and Harmony

Angel of Unconditional Love and Freedom—Angel of Service and Synthesis

Angel of Success—Angel of Materiality and Temptation

Angel of Truth and Enlightenment—Angel of Spiritual Strength and Will

Angel of Cycles and Solutions—Angel of Patience and Acceptance

Angel of Renunciation and Regeneration—Angel of Imagination and Liberation

Angel of Illusion and Reality—Angel of Loving Relationships

Angel of Illusion and Reality—Angel of Discernment

Angel of the Creative Word—Angel of Death and Rebirth

Angel of Creative Wisdom—Angel of Victory and Triumph

Angel of Courage and Perseverance—Angel of Power and Authority

Consorts: active-passive energies that need to blend in order to maximize their efforts:

Angel of Power and Authority—Angel of Abundance

Angel of Spiritual Understanding—Angel of Creative Wisdom

Angels with different energies that may need to be harmonized for joint action:

Angel of Service and Synthesis—Angel of Spiritual Strength and Will

Angel of Materiality and Temptation—Angel of Victory and Triumph

Angel of Imagination and Liberation—Angel of Discernment

Angel of Order and Harmony—Angel of Power and Authority

Angel of Death and Rebirth—Angel of Spiritual Understanding

Angel of Patience and Acceptance—Angel of Loving Relationships

Angel of Success—Angel of Creative Wisdom

Angel of Unconditional Love and Freedom—Angel of Truth and Enlightenment

Angel of Renunciation and Regeneration—Angel of Illusion and Reality

Angel of Courage and Perseverance—Angel of Abundance

Angel of Abundance—Angel of the Creative Word

Angel of Illusion and Reality—Angel of Cycles and Solutions

Notes

Introduction to the Angels of the Kingdom

1. Manly P. Hall, *The Secret Teachings of All Ages* (Los Angeles: The Philosophical Research Society, Inc., 1977), p. CXXIX.

2. Ibid., p. LVIII.

3. *Metaphysical Bible Dictionary* (Unity Village, Mo.: Unity School of Christianity, 1931), p. 52.

4. H. K. Challoner, *Watchers of the Seven Spheres* (London: George Routledge & Sons, Ltd., 1933), excerpted from pp. ix, x, xi, 19.

5. Edwin C. Steinbrecher, *The Inner Guide Meditation* (Wellingborough, Northamptonshire, Great Britain: The Aquarian Press, 1982), p. 25.

6. Challoner, *Watchers of the Seven Spheres*, pp. 23–24.

7. Dr. Douglas Baker, *The Jewel in the Lotus* (Herts, Eng.: Douglas Baker, 1974), p. 84.

One: The Angel of Unconditional Love and Freedom

1. John Randolph Price, *A Spiritual Philosophy for the New World* (Boerne, Tex.: Quartus Books, 1990), p. 61.

2. Alice A. Bailey, *A Treatise on White Magic* (New York: Lucis Publishing Company, 1967), p. 238.

3. Dr. Douglas Baker, *The Jewel in the Lotus* (Herts, Eng.: Douglas Baker, 1974), p. 60.

Two: The Angel of Illusion and Reality

1. Dr. Paul Foster Case, *Highlights of Tarot* (Los Angeles: Builders of the Adytom, Ltd., Publishers, 1931), p. 17.

2. Frances W. Foulks, *Effectual Prayer* (Lee's Summit, Mo.: Unity School of Christianity, 1966), p. 52.

3. Alice A. Bailey, *Esoteric Astrology* (New York: Lucis Publishing Company, 1982 edition), pp. 272–73.

4. H. P. Blavatsky, *The Secret Doctrine,* vol. 1 (Covina, Calif.: Theosophical University Press, 1925), p. 513.

5. Hall, *Secret Teachings of All Ages,* pp. XXXVIII, XXXIX.

Three: The Angel of Creative Wisdom

1. Hall, *Secret Teachings of All Ages,* pp. XLVI, XLVIII.

2. Alfred Douglas, *The Tarot* (New York: Viking Penguin Inc., 1972), p. 55.

Four: The Angel of Abundance

1. Frances Sakoian and Louis S. Acker, *The Astrologer's Handbook* (New York: Harper & Row, Publishers, 1987), pp. 304–305.

Five: The Angel of Power and Authority

1. Alice A. Bailey, *Esoteric Astrology* (New York: Lucis Publishing Company, 1982), p. 93.

2. John Jocelyn, *Meditations on the Signs of the Zodiac* (San Francisco: Harper & Row, Publishers, 1970), p. 31.

Six: The Angel of Spiritual Understanding

1. Emilie H. Cady, *Lessons in Truth* (Unity Village, Mo.: Unity Books, 1894), p. 98–99.

2. Alice A. Bailey, *Esoteric Astrology,* pp. 374–375.

3. Torkom Saraydarian, *The Symphony of the Zodiac* (Sedona, Ariz.: Aquarian Educational Group, 1980), pp. 81, 82.

Seven: The Angel of Loving Relationships

1. John Randolph Price, *A Spiritual Philosophy for the New World* (Boerne, Tex.: Quartus Books, 1990), p. 102.

2. Kenneth Wapnick, *Forgiveness and Jesus* (Roscoe, N.Y.: Foundation for "A Course in Miracles," 1983), p. 116.

3. John Randolph Price, *The Abundance Book* (Boerne, Tex.: Quartus Books, 1987).

4. Manly P. Hall, *The Secret Teachings of All Ages* (Los Angeles: The Philadelphia Research Society, Inc., 1977), p. L; Dr. Paul Foster Case, *Highlights of Tarot* (Los Angeles: Builders of the Adytom, Ltd., Publishers, 1931), p. 23.

5. *The Quartus Report* is a monthly teaching and sharing guide written for members of the international Quartus Society and published by the Quartus Foundation, Boerne, Texas.

6. John Jocelyn, *Meditations on the Signs of the Zodiac* (San Francisco: Harper & Row, Publishers, 1970), p. 68.

Eight: The Angel of Victory and Triumph

1. Edwin C. Steinbrecher, *The Inner Guide Meditation* (Wellingborough, Northamptonshire, Great Britain: The Aquarian Press, 1982), p. 170.

2. Manly P. Hall, *The Secret Teachings of All Ages* (Los Angeles: The Philosophical Research Society, Inc., 1977), p. XXVII.

3. Alfred Douglas, *The Tarot* (New York: Viking Penguin Inc., 1972), p. 70.

4. Hall, p. CXXX.

Nine: The Angel of Order and Harmony

1. *A Course in Miracles,* vol. 2, *Workbook for Students* (Foundation for Inner Peace, 1975), pp. 351–52.

2. Dr. Douglas Baker, *The Theory and Practice of Meditation* (Herts, Eng.: Douglas Baker, 1975), p. 283.

3. Torkom Saraydarian, *The Symphony of the Zodiac* (Sedona, Ariz.: Aquarian Educational Group, 1980), p. 210.

4. John Randolph Price, *Practical Spirituality* (Boerne, Tex.: Quartus Books, 1985), pp. 127–130.

5. John Randolph Price, *The Superbeings* (mass-market edition: New York: Fawcett Crest, Ballantine Books, 1988; trade edition: Boerne, Tex.: Quartus Books, 1981).

6. Manly P. Hall, *The Secret Teachings of All Ages* (Los Angeles: The Philosophical Research Society, Inc., 1977), p. CXXXI.

7. John Jocelyn, *Meditations on the Signs of the Zodiac* (San Francisco: Harper & Row, Publishers, 1978), p. 135.

8. John Randolph Price, *The Planetary Commission* (Boerne, Tex.: Quartus Books, 1984).

Ten: The Angel of Discernment

1. Newton Dillaway, ed., *The Gospel of Emerson* (Wakefield, Mass.: The Montrose Press, 1949), pp. 43–45.

2. *The World Book Encyclopedia,* vol. 1, "Adonis" (Chicago: Field Enterprises Educational Corporation, 1967).

3. Alfred Douglas, *The Tarot* (New York: Viking Penguin Inc., 1972), p. 77.

4. H. K. Challoner, *Watchers of the Seven Spheres* (London: George Routledge & Sons, Ltd., 1933), p. 53.

Eleven: The Angel of Cycles and Solutions

1. John Randolph Price, *The Superbeings* (New York: Fawcett Crest, Ballantine Books, 1988), p. XXI.

Twelve: The Angel of Spiritual Strength and Will

1. John Jocelyn, *Meditations on the Signs of the Zodiac* (San Francisco: Harper & Row, Publishers, 1970), p. 101.

2. Torkom Saraydarian, *The Symphony of the Zodiac* (Sedona, Ariz.: Aquarian Educational Group, 1980), p. 174.

3. J. Sig Paulson, *Your Power to Be* (Lakemont, Ga.: CSA Press, Publishers, 1969), p. 151.

Thirteen: The Angel of Renunciation and Regeneration

1. Manly P. Hall, *Codex Rosae Crucis* (Los Angeles: The Philosophers Press, 1938), p. 54.

2. Alice A. Bailey, *Esoteric Psychology II* (New York: Lucis Publishing Company, 1960), p. 107.

3. John Randolph Price, *A Spiritual Philosophy for the New World* (Boerne, Tex.: Quartus Books, 1990), p. 18.

4. Ibid., p. 107.

5. *Metaphysical Bible Dictionary,* "Water" (Unity Village, Mo.: Unity School of Christianity, 1931).

6. Manly P. Hall, *The Secret Teachings of All Ages* (Los Angeles: The Philosophical Research Society, Inc., 1977), p. CXXXI.

7. Dr. Paul Foster Case, *Highlights of Tarot* (Los Angeles: Builders of the Adytom, Ltd., Publishers, 1931), p. 27.

8. Dan Oldenburg, "Revisioning Social Science: Uranus and Neptune," *Planet Earth,* vol. 11, no. 2, 1991 (Eugene, Ore.: Mark Lerner, Publisher), p. 25.

Fourteen: *The Angel of Death and Rebirth*

1. Alfred Douglas, *The Tarot* (New York: Viking Penguin Inc., 1972), p. 89.

2. Dr. Paul Foster Case, *Highlights of Tarot* (Los Angeles: Builders of the Adytom, Ltd., Publishers, 1931), p. 28.

3. Manly P. Hall, *The Secret Teachings of All Ages* (Los Angeles: The Philosophical Research Society, Inc., 1977), p. CXXXI.

4. Alice A. Bailey, with statement of myth by Dr. Francis Merchant, *The Labours of Hercules* (London: Lucis Press Limited, 1974), pp. 67–68.

5. John Randolph Price, *Practical Spirituality* (Boerne, Tex.: Quartus Books, 1985), p. 113.

6. Case, *Highlights,* p. 28.

7. John Jocelyn, *Meditations on the Signs of the Zodiac* (San Francisco: Harper & Row, Publishers, 1970), p. 160.

Fifteen: The Angel of Patience and Acceptance

1. *The World Book Encyclopedia,* vol. 10, "Iris" (Chicago: Field Enterprises Educational Corporation, 1967).

2. Dr. Paul Foster Case, *Highlights of Tarot* (Los Angeles: Builders of the Adytom, Ltd., Publishers, 1931), p. 29.

3. Alice A. Bailey, *Esoteric Astrology* (New York: Lucis Publishing Company, 1982), pp. 180–81.

Sixteen: The Angel of Materiality and Temptation

1. Gilberto Reys, Jr., "Where Belief in Satan Will Lead Troubles Some," *San Antonio Light,* religious section, May 11, 1991.

2. *Trumpet,* Newsletter of National Research Institute, July 1987, Aurora, Colo.

3. *Metaphysical Bible Dictionary,* "Satan" (Unity Valley, Mo.: Unity School of Christianity, 1931).

4. Newton Dillaway, ed., *The Gospel of Emerson* (Wakefield, Mass.: The Montrose Press, 1949), p. 33.

5. *The World Book Encyclopedia,* vol. 11, "Janus" (Chicago: Field Enterprises Educational Corporation, 1967).

6. Manly P. Hall, *The Secret Teachings of All Ages* (Los Angeles: The Philosophical Research Society, Inc., 1977), p. CXXVIII.

7. John Jocelyn, *Meditations on the Signs of the Zodiac* (San Francisco: Harper & Row, Publishers, 1970), p. 195.

8. Torkom Saraydarian, *The Symphony of the Zodiac* (Sedona, Ariz.: Aquarian Educational Group, 1980), p. 245.

Seventeen: The Angel of Courage and Perseverance

1. Alice A. Bailey, *Esoteric Astrology* (New York: Lucis Publishing Company, 1982), p. 212.

2. Dr. Paul Foster Case, *Highlights of Tarot* (Los Angeles: Builders of the Adytom, Ltd., Publishers, 1931), p. 30.

Eighteen: The Angel of Service and Synthesis

1. Manly P. Hall, *The Secret Teachings of All Ages* (Los Angeles: The Philosophical Research Society, Inc., 1977), p. CLXXV.

2. Alice A. Bailey, *Discipleship in the New Age,* vol. 1 (New York: Lucis Publishing Company, 1972), p. 656.

3. Alice A. Bailey, *The Rays and the Initiations* (New York: Lucis Publishing Company, 1960), p. 121.

4. John Jocelyn, *Meditations on the Signs of the Zodiac* (San Francisco: Harper & Row, Publishers, 1970), pp. 217–25.

Nineteen: The Angel of Imagination and Liberation

1. Alice A. Bailey, *A Treatise on White Magic* (New York: Lucis Publishing Company, 1967), p. 472.

2. Torkom Saraydarian, *The Symphony of the Zodiac* (Sedona, Ariz.: Aquarian Educational Group, 1980), p. 287.

3. Dr. Paul Foster Case, *Highlights of Tarot* (Los Angeles: Builders of the Adytom, Ltd., Publishers, 1931), p. 32.

Twenty: The Angel of Truth and Enlightenment

1. "Paracelsus" by Robert Browning.

2. Elaine Pagels, *The Gnostic Gospels* (New York: Vintage Books, 1981), p. 162.

3. John Randolph Price, *A Spiritual Philosophy for the New World* (Boerne, Tex.: Quartus Books, 1990), p. 19.

4. Newton Dillaway, ed., *The Gospel of Emerson* (Wakefield, Mass.: The Montrose Press, 1949), p. 57.

5. Manly P. Hall, *The Secret Teachings of All Ages* (Los Angeles: The Philosophical Research Society, Inc., 1977), p. XLIX.

6. Ibid., p. LI.

7. Ibid., p. CXXXII.

Twenty-one: The Angel of the Creative Word

1. Manly P. Hall, *The Secret Teachings of All Ages* (Los Angeles: The Philosophical Research Society, Inc., 1977), p. XC.

2. Ibid., p. XC.

3. Alice A. Bailey, *Initiation, Human and Solar* (New York: Lucis Publishing Company, 1967), p. 150.

4. Charles Fillmore, *Christian Healing* (Lee's Summit, Mo.: Unity School of Christianity, 1964), p. 68.

5. Ernest Holmes, *The Science of Mind* (New York: Dodd, Mead and Company, 1938), p. 476.

6. Bailey, *Initiation*, p. 159.

Twenty-two: The Angel of Success

1. *The World Book Encyclopedia,* "Saturn" (Chicago: Field Enterprises Educational Corporation, 1967).

2. Alice A. Bailey, *A Treatise on White Magic* (New York: Lucis Publishing Company, 1967), p. 634.

3. Ibid., p. 635.

4. Dr. Paul Foster Case, *Highlights of Tarot* (Los Angeles: Builders of the Adytom, Ltd., Publishers, 1931), p. 34.

ABOUT THE AUTHOR

JOHN RANDOLPH PRICE is the cofounder, with his wife, Jan, of the Quartus Foundation, a spiritual research and communications organization formed in 1981 and currently headquartered on the Guadalupe River Ranch in the Texas hill country.

With Jan's collaboration John has authored more than ten books, including *The Superbeings, A Spiritual Philosophy for the New World*, and this most recent one, *The Angels Within Us*. They also hold retreats on the ranch and give workshops based on material from the books.

In 1984 the Prices announced the Planetary Commission for World Healing, which called for a simultaneous global mind-link at noon Greenwich time, December 31, 1986—and continuing each year on the same date. Based on computer analysis of information from sources worldwide, more than 500 million people participated on the first World Healing Day in 1986, and the numbers have grown each year. In recognition of this activity, John and Jan were named the recipients of the Light of God Expressing Award by the Association of Unity Churches. And in 1992 John was presented the Humanitarian Award for Peace by the Arizona chapter of the International New Thought Alliance.

Prior to writing his first book John devoted twenty-five years to the corporate world, holding executive positions in business and industry.